Augustus Peck Clarke

Clarke's Kindred Genealogies

A genealogical history of certain descendants of Joseph Clarke, Dorchester, 1630 -

Denice Darling, Braintree, 1662 - Edward Gray, Plymouth, 1643 - and William

Horne, Dover, 1659

Augustus Peck Clarke

Clarke's Kindred Genealogies
A genealogical history of certain descendants of Joseph Clarke, Dorchester, 1630 - Denice Darling, Braintree, 1662 - Edward Gray, Plymouth, 1643 - and William Horne, Dover, 1659

ISBN/EAN: 9783337733988

Printed in Europe, USA, Canada, Australia, Japan

Cover: Foto ©Andreas Hilbeck / pixelio.de

More available books at **www.hansebooks.com**

Clarke's Kindred Genealogies.

A Genealogical History of Certain Descendants of

JOSEPH CLARKE, DORCHESTER, 1630;
DENICE DARLING, BRAINTREE, 1662;
EDWARD GRAY, PLYMOUTH, 1643;
AND WILLIAM HORNE, DOVER, 1659;

AND SKETCHES OF THE

Orne (Horne), Pynchon, and Downing Families,

BY

AUGUSTUS PECK CLARKE, A. M., M. D.,

OF CAMBRIDGE, MASS.,

Member of the New-England Historic Genealogical Society.

"Ὥσπερ ξένοι χαίροντες ἰδεῖν πατρίδα γαῖαν,
Οὗτως δὲ οἱ γράφοντες ἰδεῖν βιβλίου τέλος.

CAMBRIDGE, MASS.:
THE HARVARD PRINTING COMPANY.
1896.

Dedication.

To the Memory of my Wife,

Mary Hannah Gray Clarke,

This Volume

Is Affectionately Inscribed by her Husband.

The Author.

PREFACE.

My first intention in making genealogical researches was to obtain authentic records for private use; being encouraged by finding entries of considerable importance, I felt that it might not be unadvisable to continue the work until sufficient material had been gathered for a small publication. It was not my design to make an exhaustive genealogical history of all the branches of the several families embraced within the work, but only to have the record extend to such members as have not received at the hands of previous writers due consideration.

In collecting such data I did not hesitate to avail myself of the advantages of records wherever they were to be found. In tracing the Clarke genealogy I followed the family tradition of my immediate ancestors, and so was quickly enabled to make a beginning that gave promise of much success. In preparing the record of the earlier descendants of Joseph Clarke I found that Tilden's History of Medfield was of considerable service; so also was Jameson's History of Medway. From these invaluable sources of information I did not hesitate to draw largely. It is also with pleasure that I make acknowledgement for the great help I obtained from Austin's Genealogical Dictionary of Rhode Island; this publication was especially helpful when preparing the record of Edward Gray of Plymouth. Raymond's Gray Genealogy furnished important data for this portion of the work.

Though these publications proved very useful, it was nevertheless necessary to make a vast deal of original research before it was possible to determine what was the connection between the families of the last few generations and those of the earliest date. In ascertaining those relations I availed myself of the direct aid of old records of the town clerks of Dorchester, Salem, Marblehead, Lynn, Mendon, Bellingham, Dedham, Attleborough, Holliston, Rehoboth, Wrentham, and Plymouth, in Massachusetts, and of those of Bristol, Tiverton, Little Compton, Smithfield, Cumberland, Lincoln, Scituate, and Barrington in the State of Rhode Island, also of those of Corinth, Fairlee, West Fairlee, and Chelsea in the state of Vermont, and of Wells, York, and Kennebunk in the state of Maine.

When preparing the sketch of the Darling genealogy, I was favored by a personal interview with Mr. John Darling of Chestnut Hill in Blackstone. This gentleman had collected many valuable records relating to this old family, and though they were mainly for his private use, he cheerfully accorded me an opportunity to copy from his record whatever facts I desired to use. Most of the dates I then gained I was subsequently able to verify by comparison with the original entries. I can now attest their accuracy.

I am especially indebted to the officers and the management of the New-England Historic Genealogical Society for their uniform courtesy and readiness in placing at my disposal important publications of their library. The courtesies of the officers of the Harvard University Library were also freely extended. Many rare volumes of the Cambridge Library were consulted with profit. Most important facts relating to the ancestors in England were gleaned through the assistance of Mr. Henry Gray, 47 Leicester Square, and of Mr. Arthur Crisp of Denmark Hill, London. I should express my obligation to the managing officers of the British Museum for opportunities to consult some rare old books and manuscripts that proved of unusual advantage in this line of inquiry.

I should not close without expressing my indebtedness to my loving and venerable friend, the Rev. Lucius R. Paige, D.D., for the loan of interesting and valuable books and papers and for kindly suggestions.

I shall not forget to acknowledge here the invaluable service rendered by my own daughter, Miss Inez Louise Clarke, A. B., of Radcliffe College; she, besides copying for the use of the printer the manuscripts I had prepared, emblazoned with her own brush for the engraver the various arms that embellish the work. Her success in this undertaking needs no comment.

In accomplishing this work which I now place before my readers it is but fair to say that much time has been employed and much money has had to be expended. The labor of gathering and of arranging the material was not felt to be a mere task-work, but was a labor of love and was prompted by a filial regard for the men who had participated in the early settlement of the country.

Inconsiderable and imperfect as the work may be, had I fully realized in the beginning how much labor, thought, and research would have been required for its completion, I should undoubtedly have shrunk from the undertaking. Now that the labor is brought to a close, I can but rejoice that I have made the attempt to offer the contribution.

Cambridge, Mass., 1896.

LIST OF ILLUSTRATIONS.

.

SECRETUM MEI GAUDII IN CRUCE

ARMS OF CLARKE.

The accompanying arms of Clarke are a reproduction of those of an ancient family in Suffolk County, England. The following is the description given in heraldic language.

Arms.—Argent; on a bend gules, between three roundels sable, as many swans of the field.

Crest.—Out of a tau cross or, three roses gules, leaves vert, between a pair of wings azure.

Motto.—" Secretum mei gaudii in cruce,"

" The secret of my joy is in the cross."

CLARKE GENEALOGY.

The origin of surnames, says Bowditch, is known to have been assumed in some instances before the Norman Conquest, but such names did not become general in England until two or three centuries later. The name Clarke, in its various forms of Clark, Clarke, Clerk, Clerke, etc., says the author of the Life of Hugh Clark, is one of great antiquity, having probably been used in Great Britain as early as the eleventh century. Like all names which are derived from an occupation or employment, it is given to very many individuals whose families were entirely distinct. To show that persons in past ages have changed their names into that of Clarke, which was considered the more honorable, the following instance is adduced. In the time of Edward I., according to an old pedigree of the Clerkes, in the Herald's College, London, there lived at Willoughby, in the county of Warwick, one Hammund, son of whose posterity (having been good benefactors to Magdalen College, Oxford) do continue still at Willoughby, being owners of considerable estates there and elsewhere, but who changed their name of Hammund into that of Clarke, as by several writings of these appear wherein they have writt (written) themselves Hammund als Clarke. One Richard of that family in a lease-note to him by the aforesaid College, in the 22nd of Henry VI., of the Manor and Tithes of Willoughby being written Richard Clerke, Esq., the descendants from that Richard for some generations downward do appear in a book kept by one of the family still at Willoughby aforesaid, and likewise in the Manorials of the said College as founders of these tithes (Burke's Peerage). The name Clarke is derived from dignities, temporal and ecclesiastical. Clarke means a learned person, one who could read and write ancient and mediæval lore; mediæval bearers of this name were proud of it; hence the present frequency.. In the "Domesday Book" Clerke was Clericus (See Lewis's Dictionary of the United Kingdoms, London, 1860).

"Clerk as connected with the church has come down to the world." "Clericus and Clergyman," as names or terms, were confined entirely to the ordained ministry. The introduction of lay clerks appointed to lead the responses of the congregation has, however, connected them all but wholly with the later office. A curious not to say cumbrous surname is met with in parliamentary writs — that of Holywater Clerks. A certain Hugh Holiwater clerk was set down as dwelling at Lincoln. As Clerk (Clerke) he was doubtless connected with the Cathedral of Lincoln; the Reformation was the means of removing the office donated. A Walter le Clerk (Clerk) is found in the same record. Our numberless Clarks or Clerks, therefore, may belong either to the professional class or to the one we are considering (that is, may be called Clerk, as a sobriquet). Chaucer speaks of "writting clerks," " Clark," " clerke," and " Beatrix Clerk." Milo le Clerk (Milo le Clark), is found in the Hundred Rolls. Beatrix le Clerk is found in the old Writs of Parliament. The Hundred Rolls* were of the 13th century and of earlier date.

Joseph Clarke, the ancestor of the Clarkes of Medfield, Medway and vicinity, was born in Suffolk County, England, where his family had long been seated. The family is one of great antiquity in Suffolk County.

An ancestor, Thomas Clarke, of Bury, St. Edmund's, gent., mentions in his will of 1506, " a Seynt Antony Cross, a tau Crosse of gold weying iij li.," which was borne in an armorial coat, and was assumed as an augmentation in consequence of having been worn by Nicolas Drury, his great maternal grandsire, in the expedition of Spain with John of Gaunt, the Duke of Lancaster, in 1386. In the will made in 1480 by John Smith, of Bury, Esquyer, mention is made of Clement Clerk for " the supuisourez of that testament; Clement Clerk is *ordeyned* and put the priour of the monasterie of Bury." The seal of the arms of the mitred Abbey

---

*The " Hundred Rolls" of England, compiled in the reign of Edward I., are records of those who owned lands in the time of William the Conqueror, for which lands some paid rent, some paid sheep, some paid hens, and some paid service as a soldier (See Driver's Genealogy).

of St. Edmund's Bury, of Suffolk, in which the Clarke family had been prominent, was *azure, three crowns or* ; " the arms of the Kings of the East Angles were assumed in the memory of King Edmund (to whom this Abbey was dedicated), martyred by the Danes, when his crown of gold through a crown of thorns (or arrows rather) was turned into a crown of glory." The Abbey was founded in 638. The arms in colors are given in the accompanying plate.

"The monastery was rebuilt in the year 903 and became the receptacle of King Edmund's body. The Abbey Church, or Church of St. Edmund's, the grandeur of which is said to have been equal in some respects to that of St. Peter's at Rome, was in the year 1095 in a state of sufficient forwardness to receive the remains of St. Edmund. It was 505 feet in length ; the transept, 212 feet ; and the west front, 240 feet. Besides a dome there was a tower. The church contained 820 windows and 300 niches, adorned with statues and other Gothic sculptures. The abbey remained in the possession of the Benedictine monks over five hundred years, the first being made by King Canute in the year 1020, and the abbot 'resigned' the abbey in the year 1539 to Henry VIII. The monastery of St. Edmund's Bury is supposed to have been only second in England for its magnificence in buildings, decorations, privileges and endowments. Leland, who lived in the time of its greatest splendor, thus describes it : —

"The sun hath not shone on a town more delightfully situated, on a gradual and easy descent, with a small river flowing on the eastern part ; or a monastery more illustrious, whether we consider its wealth, its extent, or its incomparable magnificence. You might, indeed, say that the monastery itself is a town ; so many gates there are, some of them of brass ; so many towers ; and a church than which none can be more magnificent, and subservient to which are three others, also splendidly adorned with admirable workmanship, and standing in the same church-yard. The rivulet mentioned above, with an orchard bridge thrown across it, glides through the bounds of the monastery." (See the Brights of Suffolk, pages 8-9).

It seems from all accounts, without resorting to speculation, that the ancestors of this ancient family of the Clarkes had before the Norman Conquest been dwellers in England. They had long been seated in East Anglia and had been influential in the building and management of the priories and abbeys of that country.

Tradition has it that though they were of Anglo-Saxon extraction they became by marriage connected at an early date with the descendants of Joseph of Arimathea. The story of Joseph of Arimathea is that, after the crucifixion of our Lord on Calvary, he was banished by the Jews from Judea. Joseph, in company with Philip the apostle, Lazarus, whom Christ had presumably raised from the dead, Mary Magdalene, and Martha his sister, and Marcilla their servant, was put into a vessel without sails or oars and set adrift to perish upon the sea (Mediterranean). The lonely voyagers, after having suffered much by being tossed by the rough winds and the waves, landed at last at Massilia (Marseilles), the ancient seaport of France. Now while Philip continued to preach the gospel in France, he sent Joseph of Arimathea over into Britain, with Joseph his son and ten other associates, to convert the natives of that island to Christianity. Those coming into Britain found such kindly reception from Arbiagus the King that, though he would not be persuaded by the preaching to abandon the worship of idols, yet he allowed them twelve hides of land (a hide of ground being as much, if well managed, as would maintain a family, or as others say, as much as one person could handsomely plough and manage in a desolate island full of fens and brambles; this was designated in the original language of that country as " Ynis-Witrin," or in our translation as " Glastonbury," in Somersetshire). Here they built a small church, and by directions from Gabriel, the archangel, dedicated it to the Virgin Mary. The land on all sides of this grand edifice was enclosed as a church-yard; in this enclosure Joseph was buried. At this place the twelve lived many years, devoutly serving God, and converting the islanders to the Christian faith. Some maintain that Philip did not come to France in this ship, but was there before the banishment of Joseph and his party. (See Church history of Britain, by Rev. Thomas Fuller, D.D., third edition, vol. 1. pp. 12-13). I am not unaware that Fuller and other writers have discredited in large part many of the circumstances of the story of Joseph of Arimathea, still it must not be forgotten that many charters relating to this primitive church were granted by the ancient Saxon kings. The Vatican at Rome is not wholly without ancient records of the early planting of this church. The ancient abbey of Glastonbury was founded in 605 A.D., on the site of a British church, long held to have owed its origin to St. Joseph of Arimathea, whose "miraculous thorn," which continually blossomed on Christmas day, together with the shrine of St. Dunstan, attracted multitudes of devout persons to Glastonbury in the Middle Ages. "It was the burial place of King Arthur, whose remains were many centuries ago discovered here."

Joseph Clarke was among the first settlers of the Dorchester company, that embarked at Plymouth, England, on the 20th of March, 1630, in the "Mary and John," a vessel of 400 tons, Captain Squeb, master. The company had a prosperous voyage of seventy days, and arrived at Nantasket (called by Captain Squeb the mouth of the Charles River),* on the 30th of May, ten days in advance of the "Arbella" and the other vessels comprising that distinguished fleet of eleven ships, with more than eight hundred emigrants, headed by John Winthrop, afterward governor.

---

*It is interesting to observe that other navigators had previously determined that the waters in this vicinity embrace the mouth of the Charles River. The Allefonsce manuscript determined our Cape Ann to be the Southern Cape Breton; it determined the river Charles to be the Norumbega, that is, the River Norumbega was in the forty-third degree; it was a tidal river (Verrazano and Thorfinn). "It is at its mouth full of islands which stretch out ten or twelve leagues to the sea. Allefonsce's mouth of the Charles had for its two promontories, Cape Ann and Cape Cod. He estimates its width at "above forty leagues." Of such a tidal river *there is but one* in the forty-third degree. On the maps of which Prof. Horsford speaks, where, at the same point and given as the alternative names of the Norse City (Watertown), Norumbega, Norvega, Noruega, Norbega, and Nor'mbega are found, and where Norvega as a province occurs, there is also, and in the same precise latitude, the Norumbega River. This was the Rio-Grande of the Portuguese, the Angulleme of Verrazano the Mishaum (Big Eel) of the Massachusetts Indians, and the Charles of Captain John Smith.

This river emptied into the bay that was seen by Bjarni Herjulfson, 985 A.D.; it was discovered by Leif Erikson, 1000 A.D.; it was explored by Thorwald. Leif's brother, 1003 A.D.; the country was colonized by Thorfinn Karlsefni, 1007 A.D. First Bishop Erik Gnupson came by appointment of Pope Paschall to dwell here in 1121 A.D., and to hold up the symbols of the Faith. Industries for 350 years were maintained upon its banks. Masur-wood (burrs), fish, furs, agriculture, were elements of industry. Latest Norse ship returned to Iceland in 1347. (See the discovery of the Ancient city of Norumbega by Prof. E. N. Horsford, 1890, pages 38-39). After that period the colony retrograded. It was reserved for the passengers of the "Mary and John" to inaugurate more active operations for the settlement of this portion of the country.

In the Dorchester Town Records,* under date of November 22, 1634, Joseph Clarke (his name in the records is spelled with the final " e ") and twelve other persons are mentioned as having a " grant of six acres of land for their small and great lotts, at Naponset, betwixt the Indian feild and the mill."

Joseph Clarke removed to Dedham, where he was one of the earliest residents of that town. Mention is made of him in the Dedham Records, vol. I., page 112. It is as follows : —

" Dedham, ye 28 of ye 7 month called September, 1640. Whereas, Edward Alleyen hath granted unto Joseph Clarke one acre of ye land next Vine Brook, towards the north for setting his house upon we do grant unto ye sayed Joseph one acre of ye land to adjoin thereunto for to make an house lot. And we do grant unto the sayed Joseph Clarke six acres of planting ground to be beyond Vine Brook to be set off by the aforesaid men that we appointed to perform for Henry Wilson, provide that he subscribe to the town orders."

After Joseph Clarke received from the town of Dorchester, Nov. 22, 1634, his land grant, he returned to England, for we find in the sailing list of those who, on October 24, 1635, at " ye Port of London were aboard the Constance, Clement Campion, Mr., bound for Virginia," Jo. Clarke, aged 38 years, and Alice Brass, aged 15 years.

She was undoubtedly the Alice Pepper or Peppitt, whom he married after his return to America, and after his removal from Dorchester to Dedham. Aboard the " Constance " at London there were eighty-five passengers ; but these did not all settle in Virginia. We find that William Andrews, who was among the passengers, settled in New Haven, Conn., in 1638. The entry bears no evidence that these emigrants were required to make the customary attestation of their conformity to the orders and discipline of the C ı rch of England. No evidence is on the record that they were "no subsidy persons " or " not liable to the subsidy tax," and " were people of mean condition." After the " C n tance " had exchanged cargo at Hampton Roads, and had allowed emigrants to disembark there for "James Cittie" and for other places in Virginia, she undoubtedly continued her voyage to the more northern ports, until she reached Boston Harbor, whence she returned to England.

Some of the names in the list were hurriedly written, or were abbreviated; some were no doubt changed or assumed, as was often done to avoid suspicion, the arbitrary orders, and the hateful tax imposed by the London board.

The ages of Joseph Clarke and Alice Brass (Pepper) as recorded in the sailing list kept in the London office appear to be correct; they are in accordance with the history and record of the subsequent lives of these persons. This makes the birth date of Joseph Clarke occur in the year 1597. He died in 1684. This record would show that he attained to the age of eighty-seven years. Mrs. Alice Clarke died in 1710; her christening occurring in 1623 would indicate that she also reached the age of eighty-seven years. There is no record of their marriage in Dorchester; the marriage must have taken place in Dedham, but not until after Joseph Clarke had removed there in 1640. At that date the affairs of the town were only commencing to advance; the record of marriages was imperfectly kept.

Ten years later Joseph Clarke was one of the early proprietors and settlers of Medfield, and in his will bequeathed lands to his sons, on the west side of the Charles River, afterward Medway.* In 1652 he became a freeman of Medfield. His first child born in Dedham was Joseph, son of Joseph and Alice Clarke, born 27th, 5th mo., 1642.† According to Tilden's History of Medfield this was his oldest son. There is scarcely any doubt that he came direct from Dorchester, Mass., to Dedham, in 1640. If Mrs. Clarke was born in 1623, she would have been, in 1635, 12 years old. In 1642, at the time of the birth of their first son, Joseph, she would have been 19; in 1660 at the time of the birth of Rebecca, their youngest child, she would have been 37. In 1710, at the time of her death, she would have been 87, as before remarked.

---

* See Rev. E. O. Jameson's Hist. of Medway; also W. S. Tilden's Hist. of Medfield.

† See Dedham, printed Records, Vol. I., p. 2.

The following record appears in the parish register of St. Mary, Aldermary, London, Eng., viz.: 1623, March 25, Ailles (Alice) daughter of Robert Peppit (Pepper), dwelling in the backe lane, was christened.

Ann, daughter of Robert Peppit, martchand taylor dwelling in Turnbase lane, was christened 1621, July 1. She was buried 1630, Nov. 17.

Elizabeth, daughter of Robert Peppat (the final syllable in the name occurring in this entry is spelled with "at" instead of with "it"), was christened 1619, Nov. 7. 1627 Elizabeth Peppit, daughter of Robert Peppit, dwelling in Turnbase lane was buried.

John Peppit, son of Robert Peppit, was christened 1616, April 2.

John Peppit, son of Robert Peppit, was buried 1618, May 19.

Mary, daughter of Robert Peppit, was buried 1638, September 30.

Richard Peppit, son of Robert Peppit, a taylor dwelling in Turnbase lane was christened 1636, May 26.

Richard Peppit, son of Robert Peppit, was buried 1639, October 23.

1618, January 22, Robert Peppit, son of Robert Peppit, was buried.

Robert Peppit and Elizabeth Leake both of the *Parrish* of Saint Mary, Aldermary, were married 1615, June 8. The *widdow* Elizabeth Peppit of Robert Peppit died 1642, June 24. She was a *pencioner*. It will consequently be seen that at this last date, June 24, 1642, all the family of Robert Peppit had died, with the exception of Alice, who was baptised March 25, 1623. Her father had been a merchant tailor, but had evidently died, and her mother, Elizabeth (Leake) Peppit, had become a pensioner for past military service rendered by her husband to the English crown.

In reading the genealogical record of the Grey family, as given in this volume, it will be observed that the Leake family was at this time of considerable importance in England, for William de Grey, who was seated at Sandiacre in the County of Derby was the ancestor of the Greys of Sutton, whose inheritance passed by a daughter to the family of Leake, Earl of Scarsdale.

Alice (or Ailles) had emigrated to America, for the date of the birth of the first child of Joseph Clarke and Alice Pepper (or Peppit) according to Mr. Jameson's History of Medway, was July 27, 1642. The name of this child was Joseph.

A Gilbert or Gibert Peppet or Peppett was living in Virginia, Feb. 16, 1623. At Blunt Point, Virginia, Gilbert Peppett had 50 acres of plantation land granted by Patent, 1626. Ann, James, and John Pepper are names that occur in the old Parish of St. Mary, Aldermary, London, Eng., and are placed under the heading Piper.

In the Parish of St. James, Clerkenwell, occurs under the date November 19, 1587, the name of Thomas *Clerke* (*Clarke*), son of Rumboll *Clerk*, christened. August 12, 1608, John *Clerke*, son of Thomas *Clark*, was christened.

In the pedigree given by Burke in his Landed Gentry, of De Horne, of Stanway Hall, it is stated that "Oliver de Horne, of Nova Kirk, near Ipres, Flanders, came over to Eng., with his wife in the year 1596 or 1597, and settled at Norwich." "But not well liking a strange country, and hearing of a cessation of the persecution in Flanders," says his great-grandson, "after his wife was delivered of a son, whom he named Abraham, the first in the Register of that congregation there (the Dutch), leaving his small family to God Almighty's protection, he shipt himself for Flanders, to seek a settlement there again," but in his "return was taken sick of the plague, and dyed on ship board." If this statement of Mr. George de Horne, of Colchester (b. 1662, d. 1729), be correct, the lost Registers of the Dutch Church at Norwich, commenced in 1596 or 1597. Many families are descended from those whose names are found in these Registers, such as Hoste, De Horne, Vansittart, Corsellis, Boeve, Tyssen, Turck, Browne, De Bert, Vanden, Bempde, Johnstone, and will find entries which they may have sought for in vain elsewhere.

18 March, 1578, Hans Peper v. Deventer met Barbara Heckaerts v. Antwerpen.

2 Dec., 1582, Cornelis Peper v. Deventer met Janneken Janssen v. Antwerpen.

31 Meci, 1597, Jacus van Hoorne v. Antwerpen met Christijnken Wouters v. Turnhout we Anthoni Jacobs.

8 Feb., 1590, Hoorne, Van, Marie f. Jan.

28 Jan., 1599, Wilsen, Christina uxor Jaques van Hoorne.

4 Jul., 1609, Pieter Godschalck v. Tits met Christina Schouteken, we. Adam Hoorne. (See Parish Registers of the Dutch Church, Austin Friars, London, 1571-1874.)

The Register or church booke of the Parish of Mooreton in the County of Essex, Baptizings — Anno primo regni dñe [?] ñre Regine Elizabethe A° q꜔ dñi Mill ᵐᵒ Quingen ᵐᵒ Quinquage ᵐˢ octavo, 1560.

Thoms Pepper, sonne of John Pepper the XXXth Januarie a° pdcto.

1583, Thomas Gyll and Agnes Pepper were maried the third of November a° pdco.

1585, Thomas Pepper and Joan Clark were maried the IXth of Maie a° pdco.

1562, Andrewe Pepper sonne of John Pepper was buried the last of March anno predco.

1562, John Pepper the elder was buried the third of Aprill anno predco.

1623, Thomas Pepper and Margaret Lyman were maryed the 9th of February.

1627, John Saltmersh & Bridget Peppar were married Nov: 6. Richard Peppar died 1626.

1624, Grace Peppar ye wife of Richard Peppar ye 29th of August, died.

Baptisms 1624. Joyce Peppar the daughter of Thomas Peppar ye 6 of December, 1624. William Pepper sonne of Thomas Peppar son to Thomas Peppar, was baptised May 26, 1627.

The name of Bray Clarke appears in the Dorchester Records in 1634. Joseph Clarke was thus early in Dorchester. Dr. Harris says in 1630; also that Thomas and Bray were there at that time, and that a gravestone was erected to their memory. The following is the inscription:

" Here lie three Clarkes, their accounts are even,
    Entered on earth and carried up to heaven."

(See History of the Town of Dorchester, Mass., by a committee of the Antiquarian and Historial Society, Dorchester.) On the list of the First Settlers of the Town of Dorchester previous to January, 1635, are the names of Bray and Joseph Clarke. Many of the persons on the list dissolved their connection with the Dorchester Plantation at this early date. Some came in the second emigration from England, 1635. Mr. Richard Mather also came at that date.

Thomas Clarke, brother of Joseph and Bray Clarke, came to Dorchester, 1630; his wife was Mary. He first appears in a list of 1638, in which year he was made freeman. Mr. Danforth alludes to Mr. Clarke's absence in England when his daughter Mehitable was presented for baptism in 1640, by his relative, Captain Stoughton. Thomas Clarke removed subsequently to Boston, where he became a prominent and respected citizen. His wife, after his removal to Boston, was called before the church on a charge of "lying expressions against the General Court* and for her reproachful and slanderous tongue against the governor." William Clarke was in Dorchester as early as 1638, and the family tradition is that he came in the ship "Mary and John." Mr. William Clarke removed probably to Northampton as early as 1658; this was after the birth of his daughter Sarah. (See History of Dorchester, etc.) Savage says that the name of Thomas Clarke's wife is not known. High should be our esteem for Thomas Clarke (brother of Joseph), who was one of only two members of the Legislature, the Boston representatives in 1656, that voted against the law for putting to death Quakers who returned after banishment. Dr. Harris says that Thomas Clarke was brother of Bray and Joseph Clarke of Dorchester, as commemorated in the epitaph on the gravestone as above set forth.

In the parish of Bobbingworth, county of Essex, England, there is mention of Richard Pepper, son of John Pepper. Richard Pepper was baptized the xxviij of October A°. 1588. John

---

* Mrs. Clarke never forgave the General Court and the Governor for enacting the unrighteous laws against the unoffending Quakers.

Pepper and Alyce Baker were maryed together in Bobbingworth
the xx day of September A°. 1579. Also John Pepper, sonn of
Henry Pepper of *highounger* was baptized in the same parish
xx day of ffebruary A°. 1593. The records further show that
Edward Pepper, the sonn of Henry Pepper, was Christened the
xx day of April An°. dm̃i. 1576; that John Pepper, the sonn
of Henry Pepper, was Christened the vth day of Aprill Anno
Regni Reginae Elizabethe xij° et Annoq̃ Dom̃i. 1570. In the
same parish records are found seven other names of Pepper.
There is an Agnes Pepper, an Alice Pepper, etc. Mary Pepper,
the daughter of John Pepper, was baptised the xxv day of Aprill
A°. 1590. In an index to the Pedigrees and Arms contained in
the Herald's Visitation, it can be seen that the Pepper family of
East *Cowton* Yorkshire had a pedigree and was entitled to wear
coat-armour. The manuscript is 1487, 160^b. Also the Peper
(Pepper) family of Canterbury, of the county of Kent, had a
pedigree and arms, as per manuscripts 1544 fo., 107^b, 1548 fo., 36,
as found in the British Museum.

As it was customary with the early settlers to perpetuate the
name of the locality from which they had emigrated, the name
of Medfield was given to the new town in honor of old Metfield,
England, from or near which Joseph Clarke and others of the
Medfield settlers doubtless had come. Joseph Clarke, as stated,
was born in the county of Suffolk, England. His family was
also connected with the family of Clarkes of Henstead. The
Clarkes at Henstead had pedigree and arms, and had long been
seated (nearly three centuries) in Suffolk County, England. "An
Index to the Pedigrees and Arms contained in the Herald's Visitation, and other Genealogical Manuscripts in the British Museum," by R. Sims, London, 1884, makes mention of those which
relate to the Clarkes of Suffolk County, England. They are as
follows: 1137, fo. 52; 1432, fo. 43^b; 1541, fo. 62^b; 1560, fo. 141;
6065, fo. 128; *Clarke* of Oake, —— 1560, fo. 183^b.

Clarke of Oake had coat armor, for the name is printed in
italics. The numbers are to be consulted as always referring to
manuscripts in the Harleian collection. The Clarkes of Suffolk
County, England, have often been distinguished, and have been

entitled to coat armor ; they have also had crests. This chief cognizance in the armorial bearings of a family is a higher criterion of nobility. Thus Fairbairn in his crests of Great Britain and Ireland describes those that belong to the Clarkes of Suffolk. The following is the description of the crests: "an elephant's head, quarterly gu. or." Pl. 35. 13; another belonging to a family of Clarke of Suffolk, "A conger-eel's head erect and erased gu., collared with a bar gemelle, or." Another Clarke of Ipswich, Suffolk County, " A nag's head, erased sa." In Barry's Heraldry, we find Clarke of Kettlestone, Suffolk County, "Argent, a chevron between three griffins' heads, erased sa. on a chief of the last, three mascles of the first." "Crest, an elephant's head, quarterly gu. and or." Confirmed June 20th, 1559.

Clarke of Suffolk gu., an inescutcheon between four lions, rampant or. Clarke of Ipswich, Suffolk County, ermine, on a bend engrailed sa. three conger-eels', heads, erect or. collared with a bar gemelle gu. Crest, a conger-eel's head erect, erased, gu. collared with a bar gemelle or.

Clarke [East Bareholt, Suffolk County] or. two chevrons, gu., a *canton* of the *last* charged with an *escallop* or. Clarke [of Ipswich, Suffolk County], or. two bars *ar*. over all a nag's head ar. in chief three escallops gu. Crest, a nag's head erased sa.

From the Visitation of Suffolk County, England, 1561, edited by Walter C. Metcalf, F.S.A., there is given the arms of Claxton, an important family of Chediston and Lavenham, in which appears a quartering or impaling or. two bars *azure* in chief three escallops gules with Clarke family, that is, Hammond Claxton of Great Livermore, second son of William Claxton of Cheston in Suffolk, married Ann the daughter and heiress of Thomas Clarke of Bury St. Edmunds, Suffolk County, and of his wife, the daughter and heiress of Anthony *Laurus* and of his *wife*, the daughter and heiress of——Hyallmii, and had issue. (Visitation of Suff., 1612.) The following relates to the foregoing families.

Arms : Claxton of Chediston and Lavenham.

Quarterly, 1, Gules, a fess argent, between two hedge-hogs of the second, one in base, the other in the dexter quarter in chief, the sinister quarter barry of ten of the second and azure, on a

canton sable, three martlets of the second. Claxton 2, Argent, a
fess quarterly argent and gules between three *mascles* sable.
(Kirkman.) 3, Azure three piles wavy meeting near the base, a
canton ermine (Safford). 4, Gules, a bend vair doubly cotized or.
(Gardiner) impaling or. two bars azure in chief three escallops
gules (Clarke). Visitation of Suffolk County, England, 1561,
edited by Walter C. Metcalf, F.S.A.

From the Visitation of Suffolk County, Eng., made by John
Raven, Richmond Herald, in 1612, and delivered into the office
of arms 1621, the following is extracted: Hammond Claxton of
Great Livermore, County of Suffolk, Esquire, second son to William, married Anne, daughter to Thomas Clarke of Okey (Oake)
County of Somerset, Esq., and by her had issue, John Claxton,
son and heir; Thomas, second son; Owen, third son; Thomas,
fourth son; Lyonell, fifth son; Elizabeth, Anthonye and Kather-
ine.

(Visitation 1561, 1577 and 1612.) John Songe of Ipswich had
a daughter Mary who married Janus Clarke of Cambridge, Esq.,
1612, embraced in the same Visitation. Elizabeth Tylney, Tilny,
of Shelley, daughter of Philip Tylney of Shelley, county of Suffolk, married to Peter Clarke (Visitation 1561).

Visitation of Suffolk County, England, 1561. Henry Veere,
Blakenham, county of Suffolk, married Margaret, daughter to
John Gowse or Gowsell or Gonsell, and by her had issue, John
son and heir; Elizabeth married to John Clarke of Ipswich of
Suffolk County, Eng. Visitation of Suffolk Co., made by John
Raven, Richmond Herald, in 1612, and delivered into the office of
arms in 1621. According to this visitation it appears that Apple-
ton was of *Kettlebaston*, Suffolk County, Eng.

Roger Appleton of Dareforde in Kent, Esq., married Agnes,
daughter and heiress of Walter Clarke of Hadleigh, Esq., and heir
to brother Edmond, and had issue.

Visitation of Suffolk, 1612, Anne Futter of Stanton married to
—— Clarke in county of Suffolk, Eng.

Hester Uftlet, of Somerleyton, Suffolk co., Eng., married fir t to
Henry Spelton, of Stockton, in Norfolk county, second to Admun-
desham Clarke.

Not all the Clarkes of Suffolk county, Eng., were recorders of mighty deeds. Some were reserved with metal-tongued bells to herald these deeds in most striking and far sounding tones. Here is an account of a Clark, an itinerant, and of his bells. The church bells of Suffolk county, England, 554 Wrentham S. Nicholas, tenor G. Five bells not in order.

1. Thomas Gardiner Fecit 1723. 2. (Pentacle) John Clarke made this bell, 1606. John Clarke, an itinerant, in Suffolk County, Joseph Carter and Peter Hawks were the Bury founders in the days of the Stuarts. George Clark cast a small ring of bells for Duxford, Saint Peter's, Cambridgeshire, in 1564, and a certificate (dated 1557) of the weight of the bell from Wymondley Priory shows that a bell-founder named Clark was living at Datchworth at that time. The parish records the baptism of a John Clark in 1575, probably the maker of the Wrentham bell. He is not, says the writer, our only specimen of a proverbial rolling stone. Before proceeding to the larger blocks of bells which occupy the great Campanarian period, the first half of the seventeenth century, there are three single specimens to be disposed of. The one at Wrentham is the second earliest known (1606) of a few bells scattered about here and there by John Clarke [He spells his name at Wrentham without the e], which in pentacle and shotten lettering resembles " John Dyer " and " Sam Owen." In the following year he cast a time treble for Cold Brayfield in the county of Buckingham. At Wormingham, Gloucestershire, and Rumboldeswyke, county of Sussex, he appears undated. I turn him up pentacle and all at Flitwike (Flitwick), in the county of Bedford, with the date 1608. In 1609 he cast the second at Eastry, county of Kent, and in 1613 the bell at Welney, Cambridgeshire. The earliest known bell of his is the little tenor of three at Eastwick, Hertsfordshire, dated 1601. This seems a genuine case of itinerancy, which the poorness of the bells may account for. (From the Church Bells of Suffolk county, England, by Rev. John Jones Rowe, D.D., of Emanuel College, Cambridge, England, 1890.) In regard to this it may be added that the price paid has often great influence in reference to the quality of the article. While we may agree in part with the distinguished author to whom we

have referred, it is nevertheless sad to contemplate that so enterprising a man as this John Clarke seems to have been, should have been compelled to travel from place to place to sustain himself in his occupation, on account, evidently, of inconsiderate returns he received for the exercise of his genius and for his work accomplished. We trust that the reader will pardon us for giving vent in the original thought embraced within the following lines :

> O blame not the maker, whose grief-stricken bell,
> Rings ont its laments, that he bade it farewell
> E'er yet 'twas complete. There had come a loud call
> With a few extra pounds from the chuich, that was all.
> Now regrets, that true worth is so oft poorly paid
> Shall by our rude tongues forever be made.

In what more honorable pursuit can a man be engaged than that of a maker of bells, whose duties are, as a quaint old writer has well expressed in these lines :

> " To call the fold to church in time,
> We chime.
> When joy and mirth are on the wing,
> We ring.
> When we lament a departed soul,
> We toll."

Or as Tennyson writes :

> " Ring in the valiant man and free,
> The larger heart and kindlier hand ;
> Ring out the darkness of the land,
> Ring in the Christ that is to be."

There were others by the name of Clarke who emigrated at an early date from Suffolk county, England, to the New England shores. Thurston (called sometimes Tristan) Clarke, aged 44 years, came to Plymouth, Mass., from Ipswich, county of Suffolk, England, in the ship "*Francis*" *John Cutting*, *master*, bound for N. E., the last of April, 1634. Faith Clarke, a notable virgin of Plymouth Colony, who was not originally named in the list of *customs*, at the age of fifteen years also came in the same ship. Thurston Clarke before sailing took the oath of allegiance and supremacy to the English Church. A John Clearke took shipping in the Elizabeth " from Ipswich bound for N. E. the last of April, 1634. His age was 22 years. He also took the oath of allegiance and supremacy to the English Church. According to the Hammat papers, William Clarke was one of the twelve who came with Winthrop, and commenced the settlement of Ipswich, Mass., 1632-3. William Clarke appears to have come with Winthrop from Suffolk county, England, and to have been on most intimate terms with him.

In the records of the parish of Brundish, Suffolk county, England, it is recorded that Edward Clarke and Diany Haywarde, also were *marryed* the third of October, 1611.

Joseph Clarke served in the Narragansett campaign in the war against King Philip. There is a record that Joseph Clarke received as compensation for certain service on one occasion in that campaign, March 24, 1676 — 00, 09, 04. It is also stated in the same connection that Hugh Clarke received for similar service —00, 07, 00, April 24, 1676. (See Mass. Archives, vol. 68, p. 86. See also Hist. of King Philip's War.)

Mr. Tilden says that Joseph Clarke's house in Medfield " was on the west side of South street, and the old cellar, near the corner of Oak street, marks the spot where he built. He served as a selectman in 1660, but does not appear very frequently in town offices." Joseph Clarke was an enterprising and public-spirited citizen ; by his energy, industry and good management, he acquired a competence. He greatly assisted in the advancement of the early settlement of the colony. He left an abiding influence for good on his numerous and honorable posterity. Mr. Joseph Clarke died January 6, 1684. Mrs. Alice Clarke died March 17, 1710.

Joseph Clarke and Mrs. Alice Clarke were members of the Old Parish Church of Medfield, Mass. The records show that she continued her membership until her death.

The children were : —

1. Joseph[2], born July 27, 1642 ; died Sept. 4, 1702.
2. Benjamin[2], b. Feb. 9, 1644, m. in 1665 Dorcas Morse ; settled in Medfield, and was prominent in town offices. He d. in 1724 ; his widow in 1725.

3. Ephraim[2], b. Feb. 4, 1646; m. March 6, 1669, Mariah Bullen; settled in Medfield.

4. Daniel[2], b. Sept. 29, 1647, was wounded by the Indians at the time of the burning of Medfield and died from the effects of the wounds, April 7, 1676.

5. Mary[2], b. June 12, 1649; m. in 1673 Jonathan Boyden, son of Thomas Boyden, who came in the ship "Francis" from Ipswich, Suff. co., Eng., 1634.

6. Sarah[2], b. Feb, 20, 1651, m. Jan. 7, 1673 first, John Bowers; second, in 1677, Samuel Smith.

7. John[2], b. Oct. 28, 1652 ; d. 1720 ; m. 1679 Mary Sheffield of Sherborn; settled in Medway.

8. Nathaniel[2], b. Oct. 6, 1658, m. May 1, 1669, Experience Hinsdale; settled in Medfield, Mass.

9. Rebecca[2], b. August 16, 1660; m. May 1, 1667, (1) John Richardson; m. (2) John Hill; settled in Sherborn, Mass.; d. Feb. 17, 1738-9.

Joseph[2] (Joseph[1]) also was an enterprising man. As soon as he became of age his father was the recipient of a lot of land for his son to build upon. This was a grant in accordance with the established custom of that time. His house was on Curve and Spring streets, not far from the old pine swamp, near which he erected a *malt-house*. He married in 1663 Mary Allen, daughter of James Allen of Medfield, a cousin of Rev. John Allen, who was born in 1597, at Colby, a village in Norfolk, England, and took the bachelor's degree in 1615, and the master's degree in 1619, at Caius College, Cambridge, Eng., and settled in Dedham, Mass., 1637. James Allen was received into the Dedham church, Sept. 2, 1646. By her father's will he received a house " which was the ancient house, probably, that stood where that of G. W. Kingsbury now stands." " At his death, he owned besides his homestead, a house and land at '*planting field*,' and a house and land in Wrentham. He served as a selectman, and as a representative to the General Court. He and his wife both died in 1702."

The children were : —

1. Joseph[3], b. 1664.

2. John², b. 1666, died 1691.
3. Jonathan³, b. 1668, died 1690.
4. Esther³, b. 1670, m. Thomas Thurston, 1658-1713, who settled in Wrentham, Mass. He was grandson of John Thurston, who at the age of thirty-six, with wife, Margaret, came from Wrentham, Suffolk county, England. He sailed in the ship "Mary Anne" for New England in 1637.
5. Thomas³, b. 1672, died 1690.
6. Mary³, b. 1674, d. 1675.
7. Daniel³, b. 1676, d. 1694.
8. Lea³, b. 1676, d. 1676.
9. Solomon³, b. 1678, m. Mary White, 1698; m. (2) Elizabeth Adams, 1740; selectman, trustee of the State loan 1721, and representative to the General Court, 1725; died, 1748. His son David Clarke was the grandfather of Rev. Pitt Clarke. Graduate H. C. 1790, and for forty years pastor of the First Congregational Society in Norton, Mass.; and the great grandfather of Hon. George Leonard Clarke, Mayor of Providence, and of Dr. Edward Hammond Clarke, graduate H. C., 1841, an eminent physician, professor and overseer of that University. (George⁷, Edward⁷, Pitt⁶, Jacob⁵, David⁴, Solomon³, Joseph², Joseph¹.)
10. David³, b. 1680, d. 1714; m. 1703, Mary Wheelock. "He received as his portion, the house in Wrentham, now Norfolk, the first homestead south of Stop River bridge. He and his wife died in the same year, leaving one daughter, Elizabeth, who married in 1722, Daniel Holbrook. Had a numerous posterity."
11. Moses³, b. 1685, d. 1685.
12. Aaron³, b. 1685, d. 1751; settled in Wrentham. His children were Mary, Martha, Esther, Keziah, Jemima. and Moses. Mrs. Mary Clarke died May 14, 1771, aged eighty-six years.

"Joseph³, (Joseph², Joseph¹,) was a cordwainer by trade. He married in 1686, Mary Wight, grand-daughter of Thomas Wight, who for his second wife, m. Lydia, widow of James Penniman, sister of the 'Indian Apostle,' John Eliot."

Joseph[3] Clarke settled in the north part of the town of Medfield, very near where Noah Allen now lives. In 1695 he held the office of sealer of leather. At his father's death he received the homestead in the south part of the town, and removed thither.

Captain Joseph[3] Clarke was one of the prominent men of the town, built the grist mill and carried on the manufacture of malt in an adjacent building. His wife died in 1705; and he married in 1706, Abigail Smith, widow of Samuel. "He died in 1731, his wife in 1756." The children were:—

1. Mary[4], 1687-1717; m. in 1705 Nathaniel Smith.
2. Mehitable[4], 1690; m. Timothy Morse.
3. Hannah[4], 1692; m. in 1709 John Robbins.
4. Esther[4], 1695-1774; m. in 1716 Ebenezer Turner.
5. Joseph[4], 1697.
6. Hephzibah[4], 1699-1791; m. in 1727 Timothy Hamant.
7. Thomas[4], 1703.
8. Abigail[4], 1711-1750; m. in 1730 Henry Smith.

Joseph[4] (Joseph[3], Joseph[2], Joseph[1]), married in 1718 Experience Wheeler, daughter of Isaac Wheeler, and his wife Experience[3] (John[2], Michael[1]), Metcalf *, grand-daughter of Michael Metcalf of Dedham, Mass., and of Norwich, England, and great grand daughter of Rev. Leonard Metcalf of Tatterford, Eng., b. there 1545, died there Sept. 22, 1616, rector of the parish of Tatterford, Norfolk, Eng., 1611. Joseph[4] Clarke died in 1731, and his widow married Daniel Wedge of Mendon. The children of Joseph[4] and his wife Experience Clarke were:—

1. "Joseph[5], 1719-1719.
2. Joseph[5], 1720.

---

* Metcalf is a name derived from the following traditional exploit, which, it is said, occurred in 1312 in Chelmsford, County of Essex, England:—"On a certain day his Majesty, Edward II, with many lords and gentlemen, were in his Majesty's park, where was a wild bull that they feared to encounter, but when he encountered with Mr. John Armstrong he was killed with his fist, and when Mr. Armstrong came to his Majesty, says he to Mr. Armstrong, 'have you seen the mad bull?' 'And please your Majesty,' says he, 'I met a calf and knocked him down and killed him with my fist,' which when it was known to be the bull, Mr. Armstrong was honored with many and great honors. And in token of this notable exploit he was made a Knight, and his name was changed to Metcalf." (See the History of Medway, Mass.)

3. Rowland⁴, 1722–1790; married, 1744, Hannah Lawrence, daughter of Ebenezer, of Wrentham. He settled in Sturbridge.
4. Hephzibah⁵, 1725 ; married in 1747, Gideon Albee of Mendon, Mass.
5. Jephthah⁵, 1727–1736.
6. Experience, 1730."

"Joseph⁵ (Joseph⁴, Joseph³, Joseph², Joseph¹) married, in 1739, Elizabeth Puffer.

Elizabeth Puffer was the daughter of Eleazar Puffer and Elizabeth his wife, of Dorchester, Mass. She was born August 24, 1714. Eleazar Puffer and Elizabeth Talbot, her parents, were married in Dorchester by " ye Rev.ᵈ Mr. John Danforth, Nov. 27th, 1713." Eleazar Puffer was probably the son of Richard Puffer and Ruth Everett, who were married in Dorchester, Mass., by the Worshipful Joseph Dudley, Esq., March 23, 1681.

This Richard Puffer was the son of James Puffer, and Mary his wife, born in Braintree, Mass., 14 March, 1658. James Puffer and Mary Swalden were married on the 14th December, 1655, by Captain Tory of Weymouth. James Puffer was in Braintree as early as 1651. Ruth Everett, who was married to Richard Puffer, was undoubtedly the daughter of John Everett of Dedham, a son of Richard Everett, born in England, the ancestor of Hon. Edward Everett, scholar, diplomatist and orator. Richard Everett or Everard (as the name is sometimes written) is said by tradition to have been a soldier in the Low Countries. Richard Everett had wife, Mary; they lived at Watertown, also at Dedham.

Joseph⁵ Clarke is called blacksmith, and inherited something from his grandfather's estate. In 1742, he sold out, his uncle, Thomas Clarke, buying most of his estate. He went to Mendon, and died there about 1780.

The children were : —

Joseph⁶, b. 1739. Thomas⁶, b. 1742. Ichabod⁶, b. February 1, 1745, in Mendon. Abigail⁶, b. Aug. 3, 1748, in Mendon. Josiah⁶, b. May 15, 1751, in Mendon. Elizabeth⁶, b. May 28, 1754, in Mendon. James⁶, b. August 27, 1753, in Mendon. Ichabod⁶, (Joseph⁵, Joseph⁴, Joseph³, Joseph², Joseph¹) married, March 28,

1771, Phebe Sprague, daughter of Amos Sprague, of Smithfield, R. I. It appears that Amos Sprague was the son of Benjamin Sprague, Jr., and Elizabeth his wife. Benjamin Sprague, Jr., was son of Benjamin Sprague and Alice Bucklin his wife. Benjamin Sprague was son of William, b. 1650, May 7, resident of Hingham, Mass., and of Providence, R. I. William Sprague was son of William, and grandson of Edward Sprague, the ancestor, a fuller of Upway, county of Dorset, England (Amos[6], Benjamin[5], Benjamin[4], William[3], William[2], Edward[1]). William Sprague, great-grandfather of Amos, and great, great-grandfather of Phebe, who married Ichabod Clarke, was brother of Jonathan Sprague of Hingham, Mass., Providence and Smithfield, R. I. This Jonathan Sprague, 1722, Feb. 23, according to Austin, "wrote a long letter to three prominent Presbyterian ministers in Massachusetts, viz : John Danforth, Peter Thatcher, and Joseph Belcher, in answer to one they had addressed to him and other citizens concerning the establishment of a church in Providence. Mr. Sprague and his fellow Baptists failed to see the necessity of a Presbyterian establishment, however, and in his letter he gave his views in very vigorous and unmistakable terms."

The children of Ichabod[6] Clarke and Phebe his wife, were :

Edward[7], born June 1, 1772, in Smithfield, R. I.

Seth[7], born May 13, 1775, in Mendon, Mass., married Dec. 10, 1801, Silvia Staples, daughter of Stephen Staples, of Cumberland, R. I.

Nathan[7], born May 10, 1778, in Mendon, Mass.

Lucy (or Lucinda)[7], born Dec. 4, 1784, in Cumberland, married Jan. 7, 1798, Elijah Darling, son of Peter Darling, of Cumberland.

Josiah[7], born March 31, 1786.

Captain Ichabod Clarke served in the War of the Revolution. He appears with the rank of Sergent on Muster and Pay Roll of Captain Benjamin Farrar's Company; Colonel Benjamin Hawes's Regiment for service at Rhode Island on the Alarm given ; time of enlistment September 27th, 1777, time of discharge, October 29, 1777 ; time of service on that occasion being one month and five days ; it was a march to Rhode Island on a secret expedition (See Rhode Island service, vol. 2, p. 40, Massachusetts Archives.) He also served as a lieutenant and captain in the Continental line. He commanded a company of irregular mounted rangers, which he had raised for protecting farms and for guarding the borders of the state; he served in the army of General Sullivan, protecting military stores and property; he was on duty at the battle of Rhode Island, August 29, 1778, and assisted in the evacuation of the Island. (See Yearbook of the American Revolution, 1893-4.) It seems that Captain Ichabod Clarke during the Revolutionary War, had service, not only in the army, but also in the navy, for his name appears again on the petition dated Boston, July 31, 1782, given by Daniel Sargent and others, asking that Ichabod Clarke be commissioned as commander of the brigantine, "Elizabeth." The petition was approved in Council, July 31, 1782. (See Mass. Archives, vol. 172, p. 182.) The brig "Elizabeth" here mentioned as fitted out in 1782, was furnished with fifteen men and with six guns, and was commanded by Ichabod Clarke. (See notes on early ship building in Massachusetts, communicated by Captain George Henry Preble, U. S. N., with "A complete list of the Public and Private Armed vessels belonging to Massachusetts, prior to the revolution from 1636 to 1776, and of Armed vessels built or fitted out in Massachusetts from 1776 to 1783 inclusive, N. E. H. Gen. Register, 1871, p. 363.) It will here be remembered that naval engagements continued to take place on the ocean during the revolutionary war until near the close of the year 1782; and that Gen. Washington did not issue the proclamation of peace until the 19th of April, 1783, precisely eight years after the battle of Lexington. Edward⁷ Clarke (Ichibod⁶, Joseph⁵, Joseph⁴, Joseph³, Joseph², Joseph¹) married, January 1, 1797, Lurania Darling, daughter of John Darling, Jr., of the fourth generation in descent from Denice Darling (John⁴, Samuel³, John², Denice¹), who was in Braintree, Mass., and who according to the ancient records of that town married Hannah Ffrancis 11 ᵐᵒ· 3, 1662. (His name is also spelled "Darley," in Brantree.) Denice Darling died in Mendon, January 25th, 1717-18, aged 77 years. Edward⁷ Clarke (Ichabod⁶, Joseph⁵,

Joseph[4], Joseph[3], Joseph[2], Joseph[1]) served in the war against Great Britain in 1812.

He was with General Andrew Jackson at the battle of New Orleans, Jan. 8, 1815. He died in Mexico, June 2, 1849. His wife, Mrs. Lurania Clarke, died in Cumberland, R. I., April 12, 1857. The son * was : Seth Darling Clarke, born in Cumberland, R. I., April 30, 1801. He m. in 1826, Sarah Ann Salisbury, dau. of George W. Salisbury of Barrington, R. I. She was born June 8, 1800, died Nov. 14, 1828 ; had child Charles, born May 22, 1828, died May 8, 1829.

He married (2), August 9, 1829, Fanny Peck, born September 6, 1805. She was the daughter of Joel and Lucy (Fish) Peck in the sixth generation of Joseph Peck (Fanny[6], Joel[5], David[4], Nathaniel[3], Nathaniel[2], Joseph[1]), who came from Old Hingham, England, to Hingham, Mass., in 1638. Joseph Peck, gent., embarked in the ship, "Diligent," at Ipswich, England, with his brother, the Rev. Robert Peck, a graduate of Magdalen College, Oxford, and honored with the degree of A.B., in 1599, and with that of A.M., in 1603. The Rev. Robert Peck was regarded by Cotton Mather as one of the great preachers of his time. It was at Oxford that the plan for embarking for the New World to raise the standard of truth and righteousness was first conceived. And so it was that these two brothers, though dignified with honors in their own land, came here for the cause of their Lord and Master and for the brethren. Joel[5] Peck served in the Continental line of the War of the Revolution, being a member in Captain Thomas Allen's Company, of Colonel Archibald Crary's Rhode Island Regiment, in 1777, during the campaign of General Spencer in that state. In 1778 he was a member of Captain Vial Allen's company in the command of Col. Miller.

Joel[5] Peck participated in the battle of Rhode Island, August 29, 1778; he was in March, 1780, with General Washington at and near Newport, R. I. while the French Army was there. Mr. Seth Darling Clarke resided in Cumberland, in Pawtucket, and in

---

* The children of Lurania by other marriage were Sophia, who married Daniel Jencks of Cumberland, R. I., and Robert, who married Frances Gorton and settled in Pawtucket, R. I., and Maria, who married first, Washington Vickery, and second, Horace Arnold Sprague, who settled in Scituate, R. I.

East Providence, R. I. He also had resided in Barrington, R. I., and in Seekonk, Mass. He served in somewhat different capacities, as school committee, surveyor, selectman, and in other town offices. During his earlier years he was much interested in military affairs, having served as lieutenant in the commands of Col. Nathaniel Fales and Gen. George DeWolf of Bristol, R. I., and in the State Militia of Massachusetts; he was acquainted with most of the military men of that time. He was prominent as a Baptist, having united with a church of that denomination as early as 18:0, and subsequently united with the Baptist church at Albion, Cumberland, R. I. On March 30, 1833, he joined the Baptist church at Pawtucket, R. I., and in 1835 the Baptist church at Seekonk, Mass., now East Providence, R. I., and continued his membership during life, that is, for upwards of 50 years.

He was particularly noted for the productions of his gardens, fields and orchards. His smiling face, genial disposition, and kindly heart will long be remembered by those who knew him. He was a fit representative of his pure, devoted and honored ancestors. He died in East Providence, R. I., January 28, 1885. Mrs. Clarke was also a staunch member of the Baptist church, having become a member in 1830. She died Dec. 21, 1875. The sermon at the funeral of Mr. Seth Darling Clarke, that took place January 31, 1885, was preached by Rev. B. S. Morse, pastor of the Baptist Church at East Providence. The sermon was styled, "*Bible Readings for the Funeral of a Saint.*"

The following is an abstract of the sermon:

II. Kings ii: 10. "*So David slept with his fathers, and was buried in the city of David.*"

In Acts xiii: 36, we learn that this was "*after he had served his own generation by the will of God.*"

"Slept with their fathers" is a figure of death, used about thirty times in the Old Testament.

This use ranges over about 900 years of Jewish history, from about 1520–1624 before Christ.

It is used by a goodly number of different writers living in different places.

This shows that *sleep* as the type of *death* was well-known and popular and a beautiful figure among God's ancient people.

" *Sleep* " with the added thought of *"burial"* is very suggestive, pleasantly suggestive — of *rest* — of " the rest that remaineth
for the people of God."

Luke viii: 41, 42, and 49–56.

Here we pass out of the *Old* Testament into the *New*. We
pass down the stream of History — of Bible Record — about *650*
years.

Here we find Jesus, who all things knew, using the same beautiful, familiar figure of death.

Nature was weeping and making an *ado* over a departed one,
and Christ in calm and beautiful simplicity presents the thought
that *Death* is a *sleep*, implying *rest*, *awaking*, a *brighter day*, as a
source of *comfort*, of *holy hope*, to the *afflicted*.   How tenderly he
says : " *Weep not :* She is not *dead*, but *sleepeth.*"

The sentence, *"And her spirit came again,"* implies the *resurrection* power of Jesus.

John ii: 11-14, 20-26.

Here the same figure is again used by Christ—to another company of mourners, as a source of real and solid comfort.

He hints his mission to earth by asserting that His mission to
that family was to awake that sleeper.

Then comes the added doctrine of the *Resurrection* of the
Body, with all the comfort *it* brings to mourning friends.   Sleep,
rest, awaking, rising, to a new day, soul, body.

Then comes the still more comforting truth to those mourning
sisters—to all mourning Saints, that *Christ himself is* the " *Resurrection* " and the " *Life*," the *life beyond* the *resurrection*, *the
life after* the body has come forth, the *glorious, spiritual, eternal,
blissful*, life of *body* and *soul*, in that infinite, eternal beyond—
beyond the veil.

Death is a *sleep*, and *sleep* is not annihilation, for *resurrection*
and *life follow it.*

The ancient classics call " *Sleep the brother of Death.*"

We have abundant proof that among *all nations*, in *all ages* of
history, the prevailing belief has been that there is an active *conscious existence beyond* the sleep of death.

What is sleep?

Not annihilation of a single atom, or force, or part of nature of body or mind.

Not an *absolute cessation* of any of the functions and forces of *life*, or *mind*, not an unconscious existence, as a stone exists.

Sleep merely unclasps the *conscious connection* of mind and body, of *imagination* and *will*, and the *mind* continuous in action all the while.

The *mind* is *active* in sleep, as is abundantly proved by dreams. Dreams are what the mind remembers of its own activities when partially awake, when sleep is not sound.

How active is the mind in sleep! Cut loose from conscious connection with the material, the *body*, how it soars away and over all worlds—all existences, all combinations, real and imagined. How it ranges through earth, through all worlds, through the infinite universe of God. How it *grasps* all subjects, all creations, real and ten thousand imaginary, unclogged, unchained, unwearied. With infinite scope, unlimited powers, how its movements astonish all our wakeful powers and efforts!

Sleep the type of *unconscious existence* of *annihilation!* Never! The most *lively* and *beautiful* and *instructive* and comforting *type* of continued *existence, conscious existence,* of infinite powers, activities.

Take some *illustrations* of mental activities when asleep:

Miss Hill, a schoolmate, solved an algebraic problem on her slate while asleep, which defied her skill while awake.

Coleridge composed a 200 or 300 line poem while asleep, comparing favorably with his waking poems.

A man made preparation for his voyage, crossed the Atlantic to America, remained a fortnight, transacted daily business, and returned to England, in ten minutes.

Another dreamed a long, sad life of continual conflict with a bitter foe, and at last was overcome by that foe, murdered and thrown into the cold waters of a lake. All this commenced, continued and closed, while drops of water were thrown into his face and he was waking from the sensation of a chill.

Sleep opening to us such powers of mental activity, teaching us *annihilation* of all our powers, *unconscious slumber* of the *soul !*

Never ! no never ! ! — *impossible,* absurd.   It rather with *intense force* teaches the almost infinite activities, forces, possibilities of the mind, the soul, the immaterial, unclogged soul of man.

It *more* than suggests the most delightful state of self-conscious existence and activities within the reach of our imagination, within the province of Bible teaching.

No wonder, rightly understood, it has been a *favorite* symbol of death to God's children in all the ages of revelation.

No wonder that it is said, " *David* slept with his fathers," that the child was " not dead but sleepeth," that " Lazarus was not dead but sleepeth," that the Martyr Stephen " fell asleep," that Christ presented the symbol as a comfort to mourning friends.

Don't let us be afraid of the figure because it has been wrested from its true meaning and beauty, and made to teach gross and gloomy and repulsive error.

Then comes, in the natural order, the blessed, comforting, doctrine of the *resurrection of the body* — a *spiritual* body — like unto His glorious body."   It does not clog, like this material body, the soul, the *activities* of the mind, the range and *sweep* and *grasp* of immortal mind.

Sleep, rest, awake in the morning.   Is not sleep a most beautiful, instructive, comforting figure of death ?   Especially the Saint's death ?

II. Cor. 15 : 20—" But now is Christ risen from the dead and become the first fruits of them that slept."   This is a fact of history, demonstrated beyond honest doubt.

The " first fruits " is the guarantee of a full future harvest.

Hence we read :

II. Thes. 4 : 13–18.

These verses show us that the grand, glorious, final issue of those who sleep in Jesus, is that God will bring them with Jesus when He comes the second time, all glorious, without sin unto salvation, to perfect forever his work for those He has redeemed and saved.

These sleeping saints shall be raised, awakened on the glorious morning, before those then living shall be changed.   Then shall all, all the saints " be caught up to be forever with the Lord."

" Asleep in Jesus! blessed Sleep !

From which none ever wake to weep ;" etc., etc.

"Therefore comfort one another with these words."

Surely the sleep of the Saints, when rightly understood, is a comforting truth, a state of intense, conscious, joyous activity of mind, heart, spiritual body, in the presence and service of the God of all grace.

Surely the resurrection of the body is a comforting doctrine to the dying saint and to those who mourn the departure of such to the world of the living.

Surely the Life after the resurrection, the glorious, blissful, eternal Life of body and Soul through our Lord Jesus Christ, is a comforting truth.

Surely being thus forever with the Lord, in the Better Land, in the Golden City, in Our Father's House, is a comforting doctrine.

> " Why do we mourn departing friends,
> Or shake at death's alarm ?
> 'Tis but the voice that Jesus sends,
> To call them to His Arms." etc.

" Wherefore comfort one another with these words."

Let us all serve our generation by the will of God, that we may fall asleep in Jesus.

At the close of the sermon a glowing tribute was paid to the memory of Mr. Clarke by the Rev. William House, late pastor of the old Presbyterian Church at Barrington, R. I.

The following is an outline of his eulogy :—

Rarely am I permitted to sit among the sorrowing, and listen to the words of another imparting instruction and comfort to the bereaved. I feel it to be a privilege to be present and bear my humble tribute to the memory of our dear father and christian brother. And all the more so since I feel that the departed *illustrates* all these gracious truths to which we have listened. He has been gathered to his fathers, he sleeps in Jesus, he has entered the future spiritual world of glorified life. He has experienced those joys of the true believer for which he was so well prepared. "And I heard a voice from heaven saying unto me, Write, Blessed are the dead which die in the Lord from henceforth: Yea, saith the Spirit, that they may rest from their labors; and their works do follow them."

Mr. Clarke dates his conversion to Christ as far back as 1820 during a work of the Spirit in Barrington some 65 years ago. And though he subsequently united with a sister Church in East Providence, he always regarded the Barrington Church and people with fondest Christian interest. The type of his religious character and life would be termed by some of our day as " old-fashioned." He was a *Bible* Christian. A man of prayer, and familiar with the truths of our holy religion. He was unassuming and child-like in his demeanor, and could most readily pass from secular and social topics to those of a religious character with great ease and freedom. He was fond of prayer and social worship and the courts of his God. Often when calling upon him he would say, " Elder, you will pray with us before you go." He relished religious conversation and associations, and never expressed any fears of the future.

And while never very robust, yet with care and simple habits of life, an even temperament and sustained by the grace of God, he attained great age, and performed much manual labor in his orchard, gardens and on his farms during the very last years of his life and up to a *few months* before his death.

And, dear friends, so much has God put into your present cup of blessing that you can hardly call this affliction. Your beloved father and grandfather was spared to reach a good old age; he was in the exercise of his faculties up to almost or quite the last moment of his life; he has left you a priceless legacy of a long and noble Christian life. The first time that I heard him speak in a social meeting I was impressed that "he had been with Jesus," and those impressions have only deepened as the years have come and gone. You may grieve over the loss of his society to you, but for him it has been *far better* to depart and be with Christ. And while you have promised grace for your sorrow, may you all so improve by the affliction, so live now and during the years which shall follow, that you may all meet Him in the final reunion in heaven, even as Christ prayed (John 17). that His own might be with Him and behold His glory. So may it be.

The children of Seth D. Clarke and Fanny Peck Clarke his wife were :—

Clarissa Cornelia, born in Cumberland, R. I., Jan. 13, 1831.

Augustus Peck, b. Pawtucket, R. I., Sept. 24, 1833.

Julia Anne, b. in Seekonk, Mass., now E. Prov., R. I., May 15, 1837.

Diana Amelia, b. in Seekonk, Mass., now E. Prov., R. I., Jan. 21, 1841.

George Edward, b. in Seekonk, Mass., now E. Prov., R. I., August 29, 1844.

William Seth, b. in Seekonk, Mass., now E. Prov., R. I., March 3, 1847.

Clarissa Cornelia, m. Samuel Throope Church, Pawtucket, R. I., Aug. 13, 1855.

She died in Boston, Mass., Feb. 12, 1862.

Samuel Throope Church was a descendant of Capt. Benjamin Church, a hero in the war against King Philip, the renowned Indian chief. The children were :—

Frederick Prescott, b. Sept. 21, 1856.

Arthur Throope, b. Oct. 1, 1859, m. Lizzie S. Earle, Sept. 18, 1886.

Julia Anne Clarke, m. Solomon Frank Searll, E. Prov., R. I. Nov. 3, 1863.

She d. Sept. 6, 1865.

The son was :—

Frank Elmer, b. in E. Prov., R. I., March 5, 1865 ; m. Cornelia Merrick Chace Oct. 28, 1885.

Diana Amelia Clarke, m. James Macutcheon, Nov. 13, 1877.

George Edward Clarke, m. Nov. 1876, Ella Frances Chaffee, daughter of Joseph and Rebecca (Anthony) Chaffee. Settled in Seekonk, Mass.

Their children were :—

Charles Edward, b. in Seekonk, Mass., Jan. 8, 1884.

Clifford Francis, b. Seekonk, Mass., Aug. 18, 1891, d. Sept. 15, 1891. [twin].

————— b. , Mass., Aug. 18, 1891. [twin].

William Seth Clarke, m. Mar. 29, 1875,

Emma Frances Harris, b. Aug. 24, 1857.
The children were :—
Florence Anna, b. in E. Prov., R, I., Dec. 4, 1876.
Lillian Frances Clarke, b. E. Prov., April 25, 1878.

Augustus Peck Clarke, m. Oct. 23, 1861, Mary Hannah Gray,
daughter of Gideon and Hannah Orne Gray, Bristol, R. I. Her
father, Gideon Gray, was of the sixth generation in descent from
Edward Gray. Gideon,[6] (Pardon,[5] Thomas,[4] Thomas,[3] Edward,[2]
Edward[1]), who settled in Plymouth, Mass.; he was in Plymouth
as early as 1643. Edward Gray is frequently mentioned in the
old records of Plymouth. By habits of industry and good management, says Thatcher, Edward Gray gained the reputation of
a respectable merchant. He acquired the largest estate at that
time in the Colony. In 1680 he purchased with seven others
Pocasset (Tiverton R. I.), where his son Edward b. Jan. 31, 1667,
settled.
Edward Gray m. Jan. 16, 1651, Mary Winslow. He m. (2),
Dec. 12, 1665, Dorothy Lettice. He d. in 1681.
The children of Augustus Peck Clarke are:
Inez Louise, b. June 26, 1868, A. B. Radcliffe College, 1891.
Made tour through Europe 1890, also teacher of the classics.
Genevieve, b. Feb. 14, 1870. Made tour through Europe, 1890,
completed her academic course at Radcliffe College, and after-
wards pursued the study of medicine.
Harrison Gray, b. July 22, 1872, d. March 6, 1873.
Augustus Peck Clarke A. M., M. D., son of Seth Darling
Clarke and Fanny Peck Clarke was b. in Pawtucket, Providence
County, R. I., September 24, 1833. His father Seth[8] Darling
Clarke was of the eighth generation in descent from Joseph
Clarke (Edward,[7] Ichabod,[6] Joseph,[5] Joseph,[4] Joseph,[3] Joseph,[2]
Joseph[1]), who with his wife Mrs. Alice (Pepper) Clarke came
from Suffolk County, England. He was with the first settlers
constituting the Dorchester Company that embarked at Plymouth,
England on the 20th, of March, 1630, in the " Mary and John " a
vessel of 400 tons, Captain Squeb, master. They had a prosperous
voyage of seventy days and arrived at Nantasket (regarded by

Captain Squeb at that time as the mouth of the Charles River) on the 30th of May, 1630, ten days in advance of the " Arbella " and of the other vessels comprising that distinguished fleet of eleven ships with more than eight hundred emigrants. Joseph Clarke, the emigrant ancestor, was born in Suffolk County, England, where his family had long been seated. He married Alice Pepper, as already stated. He first settled in Dorchester, a part of which is now within the limits of Boston ; later he settled in Dedham, and in 1652 " was one of the first thirteen who undertook the settlement of Medfield, Mass." He is the American ancestor of a numerous posterity, many of whom have taken prominent part in municipal, legislative, judiciary, and in military affairs, and have been successful in business, and in promoting the welfare of the community. Dr. Clarke's mother, Fanny[6] Peck, was of the sixth generation in descent from Joseph Peck (Joel[5], David[4], Nathaniel[3], Nathaniel[2], Joseph[1]), who was baptized in Beccles, Suffolk County, England, April 30, 1587, and came in the ship " Diligent " from old Hingham, England, to Hingham, Mass., in 1638. Joseph Peck, the American ancestor, was a descendant in the twenty-first generation from John Peck of Belton, Yorkshire, England, knight. This family is one of great antiquity. Joseph Peck had a large and honorable posterity. Dr. Clarke's great grandfather, Captain Ichabod Clarke of the sixth generation of Joseph Clarke, served as a Lieutenant also as Captain in the War of the Revolution, and his grandfather Edward Clarke in the War of 1812. Dr. Clarke's maternal grandfather, Joel Peck, also served in the Revolutionary War, was with General Washington, and participated in the battle of Rhode Island, August 27, 1778. Dr. Clarke completed his preparatory course in the University Grammar School at Providence, R. I., and entered Brown University in September, 1856. Received from that University the degree of A. M., in the class 1861 ; studied Medicine and received from Harvard University the degree of M.D. in the class of 1862. Entered the army as assistant surgeon of the Sixth New York Cavalry, August 1, 1861 ; served in the Peninsular Campaign conducted by General McClellan, and during the Seven Days Battles was taken prisoner at the battle of Savage's Station

Va., June 29, 1862, and later was sent to Richmond, and after much suffering was exchanged. Promoted to the rank of surgeon in the Sixth New York Cavalry, May 5, 1863. At the opening of the campaign made by the Army of the Potomac, under the command of General Grant, in the winter and spring of 1864, Dr. Clarke was appointed Surgeon-in-chief of the Second Brigade, First Division, of the Cavalry Corps, whose glorious achievements rendered immortal the name of Philip H. Sheridan. Dr. Clarke was chief medical officer of that brigade until the closing campaign, which commenced early in the spring of 1865, when he was appointed surgeon-in-chief of the entire First Division of Cavalry. These arduous labors he also performed until the Division was disbanded, July 1, 1865. During his four years' service Dr. Clarke participated in upwards of eighty-two battles and engagements with the enemy. "In the hour of battle, Surgeon Clarke," said the Division commander, Major General Thomas C. Devin, to the Hon. Secretary of War, "was always at the front attending to the care and the removal of the wounded, and freely periled his life when duty required. He was known as one of the most efficient officers in the Medical Staff of the Cavalry." October 20, 1865, he was brevetted Lieutenant Colonel "for gallant and meritorious conduct during his term of service." Immediately after the close of his military service in 1865, he travelled abroad and devoted much time in attendance at the various medical schools and hospitals in London, Paris, Leipzig, and in other great centres, for the purpose of fitting himself more particularly for obstetrical, gynæcological and surgical work. In 1866, he removed to Cambridge, Mass., where he soon established a reputation in the practice of medicine, in which profession he has since continued his labors. Dr. Clarke was married in Bristol, R. I, October 23, 1861, to Mary H. Gray, daughter of the late Gideon and Hannah Orne (Metcalf) Gray. Of this union are two daughters, Inez Louise and Genevieve Clarke.

For 1871-73 Dr. Clarke was elected to the Cambridge Common Council, and for 1874 to the Board of Aldermen. He declined further municipal service. Dr. Clarke is a member of the Massachusetts Medical Society and has been a member of its

council.   He has been an active worker in the Gynecological
Society of Boston and was the president of that body in 1891-'92,
member of the American Academy of Medicine, and of the American Association of Obstetricians and Gynecologists, and of the
American Public Health Association.   He is a member of the
American Medical Association and a vice-president of that asso-
ciation for 1895-'96 ; and a delegate to the British Medical Association, 1890.   He is one of the founders of the Cambridge Society
for Medical Improvement, and for some years was its secretary.
Also a member of the Ninth International Medical Congress at
Washington, D. C., 1887 ; of the Tenth International Medical
Congress at Berlin, Germany, 1890; of the Eleventh at Rome,
Italy, 1894 ; and of the Twelfth at Moscow, Russia, 1897 ; the member for Massachusetts on the Committee to organize the Pan-American Medical Congress (comprising the medical profession of the
western hemisphere), and was elected vice-president of the Congress for 1893.   He is a member of the Cambridge Club and was
the president of the Cambridge Art Circle, 1890-'91-'92.   He is a
member of the G. A. R. and of the Military Order of the Loyal
Legion of the United States, and a member of its board of officers
1895-'96 ; member of the Brown Alumni Association and of the
Harvard Medical Alumni Association.

After the close of the Medical Congress in Berlin Dr. Clarke,
accompanied by his wife and two daughters, resumed his travels,
through other parts of Germany, through Austria, Italy, Switzer-
land, France, Belgium, and Holland.   He also made an extended
tour through the British Isles, including London and Edinburgh.
In the various capitals through which he passed he visited most of
the hospitals, and the centres for art, and places for improvement
generally.   Dr. Clarke has visited many important sections of his
own country, and also of the Canadas, and has learned much in regard to the hospitals and methods of practice.

The following are the titles of some of the papers Dr. Clarke
has contributed :

" Series of Histories of Wounds and other Injuries, " Medical
and Surgical History of the War of the Rebellion, 1865.

" Cases of Tracheotomy," Boston Medical and Surgical Journal,
1868.

"Cases of Puerperal Peritonitis," 1868.

"Cases of Strangulated Hernia operated upon Antiseptically," 1870.

"Perforating Ulcer of the Duodenum," Boston Medical and Surgical Journal, 1881.

"Removal of Intra-Uterine Fibroids," Ibid., 1882.

"Cerebral Erysipelas," Ibid., 1883.

"Hemiplegia," Journal American Medical Association, 1884.

"Uterine Displacements," Ibid., 1884.

"Obstinate Vomiting of Pregnancy," Ibid., 1885.

"Vascular Growths of the Female Meatus, Urinarius," Medical Press and Circular, London, England, 1887, and Transactions of the Ninth International Medical Congress, 1887.

"Pathogenic Organisms," Journal of the American Medical Association, 1883.

"Rabies and Hydrophobia," Ibid, 1883.

"Fracture of the Cervical Vertebrae," Ibid., 1884.

"Induced Premature Labor," Ibid., 1885.

"Renal Calculi," Ibid., 1885.

"Pelvic Cellulitis," Ibid., 1886.

"Early and Repeated Tapping in Ascites," Ibid., 1886.

"Abortion for Uncontrollable Vomiting of Pregnancy," Ibid., 1888, and the Archives of Gynecology, 1888.

"Antepartum Hour-Glass Constriction of the Uterus," Journal American Medical Association, 1888.

"Chronic Cystitis in the Female," Ibid., 1890, and American Journal of Obstetrics, 1889.

"Treatment of Certain Cases of Salpingitis," Transactions of the American Association Obstetricians and Gynecologists, 1888.

"Management of the Perineum During Labor," Ibid., 1889, and American Journal of Obstetrics, 1889.

"Rapid Dilatation of the Cervix Uteri," Transactions Gynecological Society, Boston, 1889.

"Faradism in the Practice of Gynecology," Ibid., 1889.

"The Treatment of Placenta Prævia," Medical Times and Register, 1890, Journal American Medical Association, 1890, and American Journal of Obstetrics, 1890.

"Adherent Placenta, its Causes and Management," Transactions Am. Assoc. Obstetricians and Gynecologists, 1890, and Am. Journal Obstetrics, 1890.

"On the Importance of Early Recognition of Pyosalpinx as a cause of Suppurative Pelvic Inflammation," Transactions of the Tenth International Medical Congress, Berlin, 1890, published also in the German language in the Deutschen Medicinischen Wochenschrift, Berlin, 1891, and in the Centralblatt für Gynekologie, Leipzig (Germany), 1890, and the Am. Journal Obstetrics, N. Y. 1890.

"On the Tenth International Medical Congress at Berlin," Journal American Medical Association, 1890.

Letter on the Journal of the American Medical Association, Ibid., 1891.

"The Influence of the Position of the Patient in Labor in Causing Uterine Inertia and Pelvic Disturbances," Journal Am. Med. Assoc., 1891, and Archives of Gynæcology, 1891; also noticed in the Medical Press and Circular, London, England, 1891.

"Some of the Lesions Induced by Typhoid Fever," Journal Am. Med. Assoc., 1891.

"Parametritis, its Etiology and Pathology," Journal of Gynæcology, 1891.

"A Certain Class of Obstetric Cases in which the Use of Forceps is Imperatively Demanded," Journal Am. Med. Assoc., 1891, and the Maryland Med. Journal, 1891.

"Some Points in the Surgical Treatment for the Radical Cure of Hernia," Journal Am. Med. Assoc., 1891.

"Post-Partum Hæmorrhage ; its Etiology and Management," Transactions Am. Assoc. Obstetricians and Gynæcologists, 1891.

"Origin and Development of Modern Gynæcology," Journal American Medical Association, 1892, and the American Gynæcological Journal, 1892.

"On The Importance of Surgical Treatment for Laceration of the Cervix Uteri," Journal American Medical Association, 1892, and the American Gynæcological Journal, 1892, etc., etc.

"Diet in its Relation to the Treatment and Prevention of Disease," Journal American Medical Association, 1892.

Annual address before The Cambridge Art Circle, Dec., 1890, Cambridge Tribune, 1890.

Annual address before the same society, 1891, Cambridge Tribune, 1892.

"Some Points in a Recent European Tour," read before the Cambridge Art Circle, 1891, Cambridge Press, 1891.

Also other addresses, essays, and papers from time to time read before the Cambridge Art Circle and other special associations.

"The Advantages of Version in a Certain Class of Obstetric Cases," American Journal of Obstetrics, 1892, and the New York Journal of Gynecology and Obstetrics, 1892, and the Transactions of the American Association of Obstetricians and Gynecologists, 1892.

"Vesico-Vaginal Fistula ; its Etiology and Treatment," Journal American Medical Association, 1893, and International Journal of Surgery, 1893.

"A Consideration of Some of the Operative Measures Employed in Gynecology," Journal of the American Medical Association, 1893. "Puerperal Eclampsia; its Causation and Treatment," American Gynecological Journal, 1893, and Transactions of the American Association of Obstetricians and Gynecologists, 1893.

"Some Points in the Surgical Treatment of Appendicitis," The Canada Medical Record, 1893, and the Transactions of the Pan-American Medical Congress, 1893.

"On the Value of Certain Methods of Surgical Treatment for Chronic Procidentia Uteri," Annals of Gynæcology and Pædiatry, 1893, and Transactions of the Pan-American Medical Congress, 1893.

"On the Relation of Pelvic Suppuration to Uterine Disease," Transactions of the Eleventh International Medical Congress, Rome, Italy, 1894 ; and an abstract published in the Annali di Obstetricia E. Ginecologia, Milan, Italy, 1894, and in the Gazette Hebdomadaire et Mercredi Médical, Paris, France, 1894.

"The Pan-American Medical Congress," Trans. Gyn. Soc., Boston, 1893.

"Some Observations Respecting Tubo-Ovarian Disease," American Gynecological Journal, 1893.

"A Visit to Pompeii and to Vesuvius," Cambridge Chronicle, 1892.

"A Cavalry Surgeon's Experiences in the Battles of the Wilderness," the United Service Magazine, 1894.

"Closing Battle of the Late War," Cambridge Tribune, May 30, 1884.

"Tribute (poem) to Dr. Morrill Wyman on the Occasion of the Fiftieth Anniversary of his Practice," Cambridge Press, 1887.

"Tribute (poem) to the Memory of Dr. John B. Taylor," Cambridge Daily and the Cambridge Chronicle, 1889.

"Opthalmia Neonatorum," Journal of the American Medical Association, 1894.

"The Treatment of Fibro-Myoma of the Uterus," Annals of Gynæcology and Pædiatry, 1894.

"Recto-Vaginal Fistula; its Etiology and Surgical Treatment," Journal American Medical Association, 1894.

"Bacteria, Bacillus, Coccus, Micrococcus; how their Intoxication May be Accelerated," (poem), on occasion of the 25th Anniversary of the Cambridge Society for Medical Improvement, Cambridge Tribune, July 8, 1893.

"The Address of Welcome," at the graduating exercises of the fourteenth anniversary of the College of Physicians and Surgeons, Boston, Mass., the Journal of the American Medical Association, July 14, 1894.

"On the Relation of Hysteria to Structural Changes of the Uterus and its Adnexa," Trans. Am. Assoc. Obstet. and Gynecol., 1894, and the American Jour. of Obstetrics, 1894, and the Annals of Gynæcology and Pædiatry, 1894.

"The Importance of the State Government Control of Artificial Agencies that may be productive of Noises," Journal of Am. Med. Assoc., 1895.

"Indications for Total Hysterectomy," ibid., and Annals of Gynæcology and Pædiatry, 1895, and the Canada Med. Record, Montreal, 1895.

"The Relation of Pelvic Suppuration to Structural Changes that may Occur in the Fallopian Tubes," Trans. Am. Assoc. Obstet. and Gynecol., 1895,and the Am. Jour. of Obstetrics, 1895.

"Degenerative Changes that Occur in Uterine Fibro-Myomatous Growths," Jour. Amer. Med. Assoc., 1896.

"The Methods of Drainage now Prevailing in some of Our Eastern Municipalities Tending to the Production and Dissemination of Disease," Jour. Amer. Med. Assoc., 1896.

"A Consideration of the Value of the Alexander Operation Compared with that by Anterior Fixation of the Uterus," Jour. Amer. Med. Assoc., 1896.

"Le Traitement Chirurgical du Fibro-Myome Uterin," Trans. Twelfth International Medical Congress, Moscow, Russia, 1897.

Author of " A Book of Poems," including " Light of Evolution" and other original poems, 1896.

ARMS OF DARLING.

The arms of Darling that are emblazoned on the opposite page were furnished the author by Mr. Henry Gray of London, from his large genealogical collection. The following is the description:

Arms.

Per fesse crenellé azure and gules, in chief a lion passant argent, and in base two faulchions in saltire, argent, hilt and pommels or, on a canton ermine, a mural crown or, suspended therefrom by a ribbon gules edged azure, the Corunna medal gold.

Crest.

Out of a mural crown or, a dexter arm embowed in armour proper sustaining an inescutcheon gules, thereon two faulchions in saltire as in the Arms, encircled by the ribbon and medal of Corunna.

DARLING GENEALOGY.

Braintree, Mass., was incorporated in 1640. From its record it appears that Denice Darly (Darling) was married to Hannah Ffrancis, 11 mo. 3, 1662, by Peter Brackett. In Braintree there was also a John Darlin (Darling) perhaps brother of Denice. This John Darling was married to Elizabeth Dowman, 3 mo. 13, 1664 by Captain Hubbart. This is the earliest record of Denice Darling in Braintree. He may also have been brother of George Darling of Lynn, 1650-1670. The children of Denice Darling and Hannah Ffrancis his wife were :—

Cornelius, b. 1 mo. 4, 1663 in Braintree ; d. 3 mo. 1668.

John, b. 2 Sept., 1664, in Braintree.

Sarah, b. January 26, 1669, in Braintree.

Hannah, b. June 14, 1677, in Braintree.

Ebenezer, b. January 8, 1679 in Mendon.

Daniel, b. April 23, 1682, in Mendon.

Elizabeth, b. July 2, 1685 in Mendon.

Benjamin, b. Feb. 11, 1687, in Mendon.

Daniel lived on the East Road which extended from Milville to Chestnut Hill ; Benjamin, on a farm of his own, consisting of a large tract of land situated in what has since been called the town of Blackstone. This farm was on what was called the North Road. John Darling was designated as Captain John Darling, which title he acquired in military service against the Indians in King Philip's War. There is a record that John Darling was credited at the Garrison at Chelmsford, January 25, 1675-6, for 00-09-04. (See Hist. of King Philip's War). John was a carpenter by trade ; he became a great business man; he was granted a house lot of ten acres and admitted as freeman. He subsequently became a great landed proprietor. He gave his eldest son (Samuel) by his third wife a farm of 200 acres in Millville, on the North

Road to Chestnut Hill. The Darlings from the first to within a recent period have held most of the land, and all the water power along the Blackstone River. The first wife of Captain John Darling was Elizabeth Thompson, connected with a family of Thompsons in Mendon and Blackstone. She died April 3, 1687. Captain Darling's second wife was Anne. Had a daughter Anne, b. April 20, 1689. She married Samuel Brown, Oct. 8, 1708. Captain John Darling's second wife, Anne, died April 30, 1690. John Darling married (3) Elizabeth Morse, born 1668. She was descendant in the fourth generation of Samuel Morse (Samuel[3], Joseph[2], Samuel[1]), who was born in England, 1585. He came to America in 1635, bringing with him his wife and seven children. He lived at first in Watertown, then in Dedham, and settled in Medfield. From this family have sprung many distinguished sons and daughters. The children of John Darling (by his 3d wife) were : —

Elizabeth, b. Jan. 3, 1692.

Samuel, b. March 18, 1693-4.

Ruth, b. Sept. 20, 1695. She m. Jan. 5, 1716, Thomas Thayer of Mendon.

Hannah, b. Nov. 1, 1697 ; m. Jan. 5, 1715, ——— Thompson.

Margaret, b. August 19, 1700 ; m. ——— French.

Ebenezer, b. March, 2, 1701-2.

Mary (Maryban), b. May 22, 1704 ; m. ——— Draper.

Martha, b. March 10, 1705-6 ; m. Benjamin Thompson.

Abigail, b. July 14, 1711.

Deborah, b. Jan. 8, 1713 ; m. March 30, 1732, Daniel Wheelock.

The *will* of John Darling of Bellingham, proved 1753, is in the Record books 10478 ; —48—196, Suffolk Co., Mass.

John Darling mentions in his will his sons John, Samuel, and Ebenezer ; he mentions Anne Brown, daughter to his child Elizabeth Brown, deceased ; the children of Ruth Thayer, deceased ; daughters of Hannah Thompson, and the children of Margaret French, deceased; his daughter Mary Draper; his daughter Martha Thompson ; daughter Abigail Verry; the children of his daughter Deborah Bosworth, deceased. His son Samuel Darling was made sole executor (Suffolk Wills, Boston, Mass.).

Captain John Darling headed the petition of twenty or more signers for the setting off of land for the town of Bellingham; this led to the incorporation of Bellingham in 1719. John Darling purchased the estate at "Crooks's Tavern," which was situated in the north part of Bellingham; this had previously been called the "Esquire Bates's Place," or "Benjamin Hall Farm." It embraced an extensive tract of land. Captain John Darling died in Bellingham ye 29 of May, 1753, in the 90th year of his age. None of his descendants, as it was with the children of Israel's great Captain, knew the exact locality in which he was buried. It is highly probable that his grave was in the old pine grove not far from where he had established that charming seat for his remaining days.

John Darling deeded three tracts of land in old Mendon to Thomas Stanford, September 9, 1722. The land so conveyed by deed was on the "ten rod road to Boston." John Darling was granted the 26th of ye third month, 1684, a ten-acre lot, and another the "Doublet lot" of forty acres. He had choice to pay for it "by three pounds and ten shillings sterling, in work, or in good pay."

Vol. 33, Page 113, New England Hist. and Gen. Register says that "John[1] Thompson, of Mendon, Mass., a large landholder, who held various offices of trust there, among others that of selectman, had David[2], b. in Mendon, May 24, 1687, by wife Mercy Thayer; David[3], b. Dec. 2, 1711, d. 1757, by wife Lydia Darling; David[4], b. July 1, 1750, d. April 10, 1815; and Willis Alder[5], whose f. was born at Mendon, Feb. 19, 1779, died in Springfield, Oct. 13, 1864, a millwright, extensively engaged in erecting mills and placing machinery, who m. in 1802, Armille, second daughter of Israel Aldrich, a lineal descendant of George Aldrich, one of the first settlers of Mendon. There is a tradition among Mr. Thompson's kindred, that they are descended from David Thompson, from whom Thompson's Island, in Boston Harbor, received its name, and there is some reason for thinking this tradition may be correct. If so, John Thompson above must have been his son. David Thompson obtained in 1619 a grant or "patent" of an island in Boston Harbor, "for the peaceable and quiet possession of said island to him and his heirs forever." In 1623 he began a plantation at Piscataqua, but becoming dissatisfied, he came to Massachusetts Bay and took possession of his island in Boston Harbor, which although it has been owned and occupied by the Farm-School Company for many years, still retains the name of 'Thompson Island's.' Soon after taking possession of the island he died, leaving a son John, who on becoming of age, filed a petition in court for the possession of 'Thompson Island's,' which was claimed by Dorchester as belonging in common to that town. After a full hearing, his claim was allowed. It is possible that this John Thompson settled in Mendon."

Samuel[3] Darling (John[2], Denice[1]) married Dec. 5, 1716, Mary Thompson of Mendon. At this time Samuel Darling is recorded as a resident of Dedham. This was before the incorporation of Bellingham, which was set off in part from Dedham. The children were :—

Samuel, b. January 19, 1719.

Michael, b. 1722.

Elizabeth, b. January 31, 1725.

Ruth, b. July 3, 1728.

Abigail, b. Feb. 15, 1731.

John, b. April 29, 1733.

Rachael, b. June 11, 1735.

Penelope, b. ——, 1737.

Joshua, b. Nov. 20, 1739.

His wife Mary d. before her husband.

He afterward m. Mrs. Thomasin Ellis a widow. The *will* of Samuel Darling is dated 1774 and is found in Suffolk Wills, Boston, Mass. The *will* is numbered 15,616. The will found in vol. 73, page 569, is that of Samuel Darling of Bellingham (then a part of Suffolk Co.). He gives to his beloved wife Thomasin (Ellis) (not his first wife) two cows over and above the contract which was mutually agreed upon before marriage. He gives to his three sons, Samuel, Michael, and John, all his land on the south side of the lands which he gave to his son Joshua Darling. He gives to his son Joshua all his homestead lands lying to the

north of the land he had given him by a deed, with all the buildings thereon. He gave unto his beloved daughter Penelope Darling a share. His five daughters are mentioned viz.: — Elizabeth,
Ruth Pitts, Abigail Draper, Rachael Darling and Penelope Darling. His son Samuel Darling is made sole executor. Probate
and letters. Warrant for an inventory. Proved Boston, April
15, 1774. On a little reflection this disposition of his property
will appear to be a just one, for his second wife, Mrs. Thomasin
Ellis, had seven children. Had he married her without an agree-
ment as to the final disposition of his estate, his dutiful and
respectable children would have suffered loss in their rightful
share of his property,

His son Samuel[4] (Samuel[3], John[2], Denice[1]), married January 20,
1755, Esther Slack of Attleborough. The marriage took place in
Cumberland. Nathaniel Cook, elder, officiated. It is recorded in
Cumberland, R. I., Feb. 2, 1764, and witnessed by John Cook,
Town Clerk. Their children were :—

Joshua, b. Dec. 27, 1756.
Samuel, b. August 8, 1759.
Benjamin, b. July 4, 1761.
Reuben, b. April 12, 1763.
Esther, b. Sept. 1, 1765.
Olive, b. June 30, 1769.
Ziba, b. Sept. 19, 1767.
Nathan, b. May 10, 1770.
Lucy, b. August 15, 1772.
Sarah, b. April 25, 1774.
Rhoda, b. Sept. 24, 1776.

John Darling[4], son of Samuel (Samuel[3], John[2], Denice[1]), settled
in Cumberland, R. I. He married Martha (or Margaret, as it is
sometimes written,) Cooke. He was called John Darling, junior,
in the Cumberland records, because there was another John Darling who was somewhat older. This John Darling was son of
Ebenezer (Ebenezer[3], John[2], Denice[1]), and Abigail Darling born
in Bellingham, Nov. 7, 1729. This John Darling, son of Ebenezer,
married Anne Jilson of Cumberland. The publishment of their
marriage was in Bellingham, April 5, 1755, and their marriage

took place in Cumberland, Dec. 4, 1755. They had eleven children. The names of these two John Darlings have occasionally been confounded. For the correctness of my data given here 1 have before me the records of Cumberland and of Bellingham relating to their publishments and to their marriages.

John Darling[4], son of Samuel[3], (John[2], Denice[1]), married Feb. 23, 1748-9, Margaret Cooke, then living in Smithfield, R. I. The publishment of the intended marriage was made Feb. 2, 1748, in Mendon, where John Darling resided. "Margery," "Margaret," or "Martha," as her name has variously been written, was a descendant of Walter Cooke[1], who was a resident in Weymouth, Mass., in 1643, and who was admitted freeman in 1653.

Among his sons were :—

Ebenezer[2].

Walter[2], died January 5, 1695.

Nicholas[2].

John[2].

Walter[2] Cook m. Catherine, Feb. 3, 1659. He removed to Mendon, Mass., in 1663. He had Samuel[3], John[3], Nicholas[3], Elizabeth[3]; Elizabeth m. Peter Aldrich.

Samuel[3] (Walter[2] Walter[1]), m. Lydia. He lived on the Mendon road near the Rhode Island line; he was a mason by trade. The children were :—

Experience[4], b. July 5, 1682.

Ebenezer[4], b. Oct. 28, 1684.

Lydia[4], b. March 18, 1687.

Hannah[4], b. Sept. 29, 1695.

Samuel[4], b. July 11, 1698.

Walter[4], b. March 18, 1701.

John[2], (Walter[1] Cook) m. Naomi Thayer : he lived in Uxbridge, Mass., and had :—

John[3], b. Jan. 27, 1685.

Jonathan[3], b. Feb. 27, 1686.

Catherine[3], b. Aug. 3, 1687.

Naomi[3], b. March 13, 1693.

Nicholas[2] (Walter[1]) m. Joanna Rockwood ; he lived in what is now Blackstone.

The children were : —

Josiah[2] Cook, b. Aug. 29, 1685.

Nicholas[3], b. June 10, 1687.

Johannah[3], b. Feb. 13, 1689.

Mary[3], b. Oct. 9, 1690.

Ann[3], b. March 4, 1695.

Daniel[3], b. Aug. 18, 1703.

David[3], b. Nov. 15, 1705.

Abigail[3], b. Oct. 4, 1707.

Noah[3], b. ——— 1710, d. 1771.

Ebenezer[4] (Samuel[3], Walter[2], Walter[1]) Cooke, m. first, Huldah Hayward.

They lived where the " Social " has been. He later, after disposing of his estate to the Arnolds, removed to what is now called Burrillville. The children were : —

Sarah[5] b. July 24, 1711.

Elijah[5], b. April 5, 1713.

Benjamin[5], b. June 5, 1715.

Elisha[5], b. April 21, 1717.

Huldah[5], b. Oct. 26, 1719.

Ebenezer[5], b. June 15, 1722.

Ebenezer[4], m. second, Experience.

The children by the second marriage were : —

Nicholas[5], b. Dec. 10, 1727.

Amos[5], b. Sept. 9, 1732.

Experience[5], b. Sept. 8, 1734.

Samuel[5], b. Oct. 8, 1735.

Silas[5], b. Aug. 8, 1736.

Sarah[5], b. Dec. 10, 1740.

Dorcas[5], b. June 26, 1746.

Walter[4] (Samuel[3], Walter[2], Walter[1]) Cook married *Margaret* Corbett.

The children were : —

Ichabod[5], b. Oct. 15, 1727.

Mercy[5], b. Oct. 31, 1728.

Rachel[5], b. Oct. 23, 1730.

Margery[5], b. Aug. 18, 1734.

Hannah[5], b. Sept. 18, 1743.

John[4] Darling, Jr., (Samuel[3], John[2], Denice[1]) after some years removed to Cumberland, R. I., where he had by his wife ("Margery," "Margaret," or " Martha," as her name has been differently written) :

Parmelia[5], b .Oct. 5, 1766.

Martha[5], b. Sept. 14, 1768.

John[5], b. August 12, 1770.

Lurania[5], b. Jan. 2, 1772.

James[5], b. Aug. 20, 1773.

Gideon[5], b. Nov. 5, 1777.

Joshua[5], b. March 5, 1781.

Jacob[5], b. Feb. 14, 1785.

Lurania[5] Darling (John[4], Samuel[3], John[2], Denice[1]) married, January 1, 1797, Edward[7] Clarke (Ichabod[6], Joseph[5], Joseph[4] Joseph[3], Joseph[2], Joseph[1]).

Deacon Peter[3] Darling of Cumberland was son of Benjamin of Mendon and Mehetabel (Benjamin[2], Denice[1]) b. June 12, 1720. He had large estates. The late Seth Darling Clarke spoke of him as a man who was held in much esteem. He d. May 16, 1818, aged nearly 98 years; his will was admitted June 20, 1818. He was buried in the cemetery near the Old Ballou Meeting House in Cumberland. The children of this Peter[3] Darling and his wife Priscilla were :

Stephen[4], b. May 6, 1750; d. Oct. 11, 1756.

Richard[4], b. Sept. 16, 1753; d. Oct. 7, 1756.

Peter[4], b. in Cumberland, Aug. 22, 1757; m. Jan. 1, 1778, Jerusha, d. of Samuel[4] Darling of Bellingham and Esther Slack of Attleboro, who were m. Jan. 20, 1755 (Samuel[3], John[2], Denice[1]). Peter[4] was a soldier in R. I. troops, 1776 he d. Nov. 13, 1796. Jerusha Darling, the soldier's widow, admin. estate, val. only $168.87

The children of the above named Peter[3] Darling and Anne his second wife were :

Darius, b. May 21, 1769.

Luke, b. July 21, 1770.

Anne, b. August 2, 1771 ; d. March 1, 1772.

Elijah, b. July 10, 1773.

Benjamin, b. July 23, 1774.

Joanna, b. Jan. 3, 1776.

Peter[3] Darling by the m. of his second wife, " Anne," " Anna," or " Hannah " Cooke, who was sister to " Margery," " Margaret," or " Martha" before mentioned, became great uncle or " old uncle," to Seth Darling Clarke. The m. of Peter's son Elijah to Lucy Clarke, dau. of Ichabod Clarke and sister to Edward Clarke, conferred upon Peter[3] Darling the same title of " great uncle." (George Darling of Lynn, 1650-'70 had Joseph, b. March, 1667, was of Marblehead, 1674; had also Lewis and Dana). John of Fairfield, m. Eliza, d. of James Beers the first.

The other persons in Cumberland by the name of Darling were the children of Joseph Darling and Bathsheba his wife :

Bathsheba, b. Jan. 30, 1752.

Phebe, b. Dec. 10, 1753.

Ebenezer, b. Jan. 2, 1760.

Lucy, b. July 3, 1764.

The next is from the burying ground of the Old Ballou Meeting House, so called. " In memory of Mr. James Darling, who died November, 1770, in the 25th year of his age." Mr. P. F. Kinion, Town Clerk of Cumberland, has kindly furnished me with the following lists of marriages : —

Timothy Darling and Ruth Darling, both of Cumberland, were joined in matrimony July 9th, 1750, by Nathan Cook, Elder. Recorded February 2, 1764, John Dexter, Town Clerk.

John Darling of Bellingham and Anne Jillson of Cumberland, were married December 4, 1755, by Nathan Cook, Elder. Recorded Feb. 2, 1764, by John Dexter, Town Clerk.

Samuel Darling and Esther Slack, the one of Bellingham, the other of Attleborough, were married January 20, 1755, by Nathan Cook, Elder. Recorded Feb. 2nd, 1764, by John Dexter, Town Clerk.

Joseph Darling and Bathsheba Curran, both of Cumberland, were married August 26, 1750, by Samuel Bartlett, Justice of the Peace. Recorded April 3, 1765. Witness John Dexter, Town Clerk.

Peter Darling and Anna Cooke were married June 12, A. D.

1768 by Nathaniel Cook, Elder. Recorded Feb. 17, 1769, by John Dexter, Town Clerk.

I hereby certify that Peter Darling, Esq., son of Richard Darling and Amey Wilkinson, daughter of Jeremiah Wilkinson, both of Cumberland, were lawfully joined together in marriage in Cumberland on the 20th day of August, 1772, by me, Abner Ballou, Elder. Recorded Feb. 20, 1773, by John Dexter, Town Clerk.

I do hereby certify that Elias* Darling of Cumberland, son of John Darling, and Nancy Alexander of said Cumberland, daughter of Anna Allison was (were) lawfully joined together in marriage on the thirty-first day of December, Annoque Domini 1789, by me, Simon Wilkinson, Justice of the Peace. Recorded Jan. 30, 1790. John Dexter, Town Clerk.

I hereby certify that Benjamin Darling of Bellingham and Celina Clark of Wrentham was (were) lawfully joined together in marriage at Cumberland on the 23 day of March, A. D. 1794, by me, Jotham Carpenter, Justice of the Peace. Recorded March 24, 1794, per Jotham Carpenter, Town Clerk.

I hereby certify that Mr. John Darling, Jun., son of Mr. John Darling, and Mrs. Ester (Esther) Mason, daughter of Mr. Timothy Mason, both of Cumberland, were lawfully joined together in marriage at said Cumberland on the 18th day of October, A.D. 1795, by me, Jotham Carpenter, justice of the Peace. Recorded October 18, 1795, per Jotham Carpenter, Town Clerk.

I hereby certify that Mr. Ziba Darling of Bellingham and Mrs. Diana Freeman, widow, of Cumberland was (were) lawfully joined together in marriage at Cumberland on the 24th day of July, A. D. 1796, by me, Jotham Carpenter, Justice of the Peace. Recorded July 27, A. D. 1796, Jotham Carpenter, Town Clerk.

I hereby certify that Mr. Elijah Darling, son of Peter Darling, Esq., and Mrs. Lucy Clark, daughter of Mr. Ichabod Clarke, both of Cumberland, were lawfully joined together in marriage at said Cumberland, on the seventh day of January, A. D. 1798, by me Jotham Carpenter, justice of the Peace. Recorded January 7, A. D. 1798, by Jotham Carpenter, Town Clerk.

---

* Elias Darling was a son of John Darling, Jr., and Martha (or Margaret) his wife, though not mentioned in the record of Cumberland births. The John Darling, Jr., mentioned in this note is the John Darling, father of John Darling, Jun., recorded in the lines nineteen and twenty of the text above.

I hereby certify that Mr. Benjamin Darling, son of Peter Darling, Esq., and Mrs. Lavina Jillson, daughter of Mr. Nathan Jillson, and both of Cumberland was (were) lawfully joined together in said Cumberland on the 18th day of November, A. D. 1778, by me, Jotham Carpenter, Justice of the Peace. Recorded December 1, 1798. Attest, Jotham Carpenter, Town Clerk.

The following record relating to the Darlings of Mendon was kindly furnished me by Mr. David Adams, town clerk of Mendon :

Samuel Darling of Dedham and Mary Thompson of Mendon, married Dec. 5, 1716.

John Thayer and Abigail Darling, both of Mendon, married July 27, 1727.

Daniel Darling of Mendon and Mary Hunt of Smithfield, married September 7, 1732.

Daniel Wheelock of Uxbridge and Deborah Darling of Mendon, married March 30, 1732.

Benjamin Meadberry of Smithfield and Elizabeth Darling of Mendon, married December 8, 1748.

Thomas Darling and Rachael White, both of Mendon, married December 14, 1749.

Benjamin Darling and Susanna White, both of Mendon, married April 17, 1760.

Stephen Darling and Prudence White, both of Mendon, married December 25, 1760.

Peter Holbrook of Uxbridge and Lydia Darling of Mendon, married May 27, 1761.

Noble Boggs of Uxbridge and Mary Darling of Mendon, married November 30, 1768.

Jeptha Clarke and Rhoda Darling of Mendon, married December 1, 1768.

Thomas Scaben of Uxbridge and Sarah Darling of Mendon, married December 22, 1768.

Stephen Hilyard and Joanna Darling, both of Mendon, married April 13, 1769.

Elijah Darling and Sarah Washburn, both of Mendon, married April 13, 1769.

John Hunt, a transient person, and Deborah Darling of Mendon, married November 8, 1770.

Reuben Holbrook and Rachael Darling, both of Mendon, married March 27, 1777.

Joseph Enos of Smithfield and Jemima Darling of Mendon, married March 11, 1779.

Benjamin Carvell and Anna Darling, both of Mendon, married September 6, 1779.

James Albee of Uxbridge and Rachael Darling of Mendon, married Feb. 1, 1787.

Pelatiah Darling, Jr., and Phila Taft, both of Mendon, married July 22, 1790.

John Darling, Jr., and Polly Warfield, both of Mendon, married June 3, 1790.

John Darling and Elizabeth Warfield, both of Mendon, married Jan. 20, 1791.

Nathan Darling and Polly Young, both of Mendon, married April 6, 1794.

Benson Darling and Lois Albee, both of Mendon, married Nov. 29, 1798.

Daniel Darling and Patience Aldrich, both of Mendon, married June 20, 1799.

Daniel Darling and Hannah Aldrich, both of Mendon, married April 9, 1801.

David Buxton of Smithfield and Philadelphia Darling of Mendon, married Dec. 30, 1804.

Seth Darling of Wrentham and Susannah Clarke of Mendon, married Jan. 2, 1814.

John Darling and Laura Anderson, both of Mendon, married April 6, 1817.

Jesse Darling and Sally Gatchell, both of Mendon, married Aug. 16, 1818.

James Darling and Mary Seargent, both of Mendon, married April 1, 1820.

Samuel Darling and Sylvia Taft, both of Mendon, married Oct. 1, 1820.

Atwood Cady and Urana Darling, both of Mendon, married Aug. 18, 1822.

Abraham Cocker and Deborah Darling, both of Mendon, married May 16, 1824.

Daniel F. Darling and Lucy Kilburn, both of Mendon, married Aug. 22, 1824.

John Pickering of Mendon and Freelove Darling of Smithfield, married Sept. 3, 1823.

Jonathan W. Thayer and Polly Darling, both of Mendon, married Dec. 11, 1823.

Charles D. Hudson of Northbridge and Sally Darling of Mendon, married Sept. 15, 1825.

Lewis Darling and Betsey Handy, both of Mendon, married April 11, 1826.

Samuel Darling and Sarah White, both of Mendon, intend marriage, date April 1, 1746.

David Burthen of Uxbridge and Elizabeth Darling of Mendon, intend marriage, date Aug. 16, 1746.

Joseph Albee of Uxbridge and Ruth Darling of Mendon, intend marriage, date ——, 1744.

John Darling of Mendon and *Margaret Cook*, living in Smithfield, intend marriage Feb. 2, 1748.

Mathew Darling of Mendon and Hannah Emerson of Uxbridge, married Oct. 29, 1767.

Simeon Darling of Mendon and Anna Phelps of Northampton, married June 24, 1784.

Jeremiah Crooks of Mendon and Phebe Darling of Bellingham, married Dec. 9, 1787.

Ebenezer Darling, son of Denice Darling and Anna, wife, born Jan. 8, 1679.

Daniel Darling, son of Denice Darling and Hannah, wife, born Apr. 23, 1682.

Elizabeth Darling, dau. of Denice Darling and Hannah, wife, born July 2, 1685.

Benjamin Darling, son of Denice Darling and Hannah, wife, born Feb. 11, 1687.

John Darling, son of John Darling and Elizabeth, wife, born Apr. 1, 1687.

Elizabeth Darling, dau. of John Darling and Elizabeth, wife, born Jan. 3, 1692.

Samuel Darling, son of John Darling and Elizabeth, wife, born March 18, 1693.

Ruth Darling, dau. of John Darling and Elizabeth, wife, born Sept. 20, 1695.

Hannah Darling, dau. of John Darling and Elizabeth, wife, born Nov. 1, 1697.

Margaret Darling, dau. of John Darling and Elizabeth, wife, born Aug. 19, 1700.

Ebenezer Darling, son of John Darling and Elizabeth, wife, born March 2, 1701-2.

Mary Darling, dau. of John Darling and Elizabeth, wife, born May 22, 1704.

Martha Darling, dau. of John Darling and Elizabeth, wife, born March 10, 1705-6.

Rachel Darling, son of John Darling and Elizabeth, wife, born May 14, 1711.

Abigail Darling, son of John Darling and Elizabeth, wife, born July 14, 1708.

Deborah Darling, son of John Darling and Elizabeth, wife, born Jan. 8, 1713.

Anna Darling, dau. of John Darling and Anna, wife, born April 20, 1689.

Mary Darling, dau. of Cornelius Darling and Mary, wife, born Dec. 13, 1695.

Uranah Darling, dau. of Benson Darling and Lois, wife, born April 14, 1799.

Samuel Darling, son of Benson Darling and Lois, wife, born Dec. 18, 1801.

Simon Darling, son of Benson Darling and Lois, wife, born Feb. 8, 1803.

Artemas Darling, son of Benson Darling and Lois, wife, born April, 21, 1807.

Jerusha Darling, dau. of Joseph Darling and Jerusha, wife, born Mar. 15, 1761.

Ichabod Darling, son of Joseph Darling and Jerusha, wife, born June 1, 1764.

Joseph Darling, son of Joseph Darling and Mary, wife, born April 6, 1736.

Stephen Darling, son of Joseph Darling and Mary, wife, born August 21, 1738.

Lydia Darling, dau. of Joseph Darling and Mary, wife, born April 21, 1743.

Enoch Darling, son of Joseph Darling and Mary, wife, born July 8, 1746.

Elijah Darling, son of Joseph Darling and Mary, wife, born May 19, 17—.

Levi Darling, son of Joseph Darling, Jr., and Sarah Thayer, born Dec. 28, 1757.

Rhoda Darling, dau. of Thomas Darling and Rachael, wife, born May 8, 1750.

Joanna Darling, dau. of Thomas Darling and Rachael, wife, born Feb. 1, 1752.

Rachael Darling, dau. of Thomas Darling and Rachael, wife, born May 1, 1755.

Prudence Darling, dau. of Thomas Darling and Rachael, wife, born Sept. 28, 1757.

Simeon Darling, son of Thomas Darling and Rachael, wife, born March 21, 1760.

Seth Darling, son of Thomas Darling and Rachael, wife, born March 21, 1764.

Benjamin Darling, son of Thomas Darling and Rachael, wife, born Feb. 28, 1766.

Alpheus Darling, son of Thomas Darling and Rachael, wife, born Nov. 9, 1773.

John Darling, son of Thomas Darling and Rachael, wife, born June 9, 1768.

Olive Darling, dau. of Mathew Darling and Hannah, wife, born Nov. 20, 1768.

Bethany Darling, dau. of Mathew Darling and Hannah, wife, born Feb. 17, 1771.

Phebe Darling, dau. of Mathew Darling and Hannah, wife, born Aug. 1, 1774.

Olive Darling, dau. of Mathew Darling and Hannah, wife, born June 23, 1776.

Daniel Darling, son of Mathew Darling and Hannah, wife, born April 1, 1779.

Hannah Darling, dau. of Mathew Darling and Hannah, wife, born Jan. 1, 1783.

Sarah Darling, dau. of Mathew Darling and Hannah, wife, born May 21, 1786.

Mary Darling, dau. of Mathew Darling and Hannah, wife, born Sept. 8, 1792.

Abigail Darling, dau. of Daniel Darling and Lydia, wife, born Oct. 11, 1706.

Daniel Darling, son of Daniel Darling and Lydia, wife, born March 28, 1709.

Lydia Darling, dau. of Daniel Darling and Lydia, wife, born Jan. 5, 1711.

Samuel Darling, son of Daniel Darling and Lydia, wife, born March 18, 1714-15.

Susannah Darling, dau. of Daniel Darling and Lydia, wife, born Aug. 2, 1717.

Kezia Darling, dau. of Daniel Darling and Lydia, wife, born Nov. 30, 1719.

Peter Darling, son of Daniel Darling and Lydia, wife, born Aug. 12, 1722.

William Darling, son of Daniel Darling and Lydia, wife, born Jan. 15, 1730-1.

Abner Darling, son of Daniel Darling and Mary, wife, born March 7, 1733.

Hannah Darling, daughter of John Darling, Jr., and Hannah, wife, born March 26, 1710.

Elizabeth Darling, daughter of John Darling, Jr., and Hannah, wife, born Nov. 7, 1712.

Mary Darling, daughter of John Darling, Jr., and Hannah, wife, born March 2, 1713-14.

John Darling, son of John Darling, Jr., and Hannah, wife, born Dec. 1, 1717.

Pelatiah Darling, son of John Darling, Jr., and Hannah, wife, born Feb. 28, 1720-1.

Ruth Darling, daughter of John Darling, Jr., and Hannah, wife, born July 1, 1726.

Margaret Darling, daughter of John Darling, Jr., and Hannah, wife, born Jan. 12, 1723.

Pardon Darling, son of John Darling, Jr., and Elizabeth, wife, born March 17, 1791.

Seth Darling, son of John Darling Jr., and Elizabeth, wife, born Dec. 26, 1792.

John Warfield Darling, son of John Darling, Jr., and Elizabeth, wife, born, Nov. 12, 1794.

Edward Darling, son of John Darling, Jr., and Elizabeth, wife, born March 27, 1797.

Leonard Darling, son of John Darling, Jr., and Elizabeth, wife, born May 15, 1799.

Elatham Darling, son of Jesse Darling and Hannah, wife, born April 30, 1773.

James Darling, son of Jesse Darling and Hannah, wife, born June 18, 1788.

Nancy Darling, daughter of Enoch Darling and Elizabeth, wife, born Feb. 15, 1769.

Mehitable Darling, daughter of Benjamin Darling and Mehitable, wife, born Nov. 10, 1709.

Deborah Darling, daughter of Benjamin Darling and Mehitable, wife, born April 22, 1711.

Benjamin Darling, son of Benjamin Darling and Mehitable, wife, born March 15, 1714.

Ebenezer Darling, son of Benjamin Darling and Mehitable, wife, born August 25, 1718.

Peter Darling, son of Benjamin Darling and Mehitable, wife, born June 12, 1720.

Hannah Darling, daughter of Benjamin Darling and Mehitable, wife, born March 25, 1722.

Abigail Darling, daughter of Benjamin Darling and Mehitable, wife, March 15, 1724.

Elizabeth Darling, daughter of Benjamin Darling and Mehitable, wife, born April 11, 1729.

Thomas Darling, son of Benjamin Darling and Mehitable, wife, born May 7, 1730.

Anna Darling, daughter of Benjamin Darling and Susannah, wife, born June 22, 1761.

Mary Darling, daughter of Pelatiah Darling and Elizabeth, wife, born May 14, 1745.

Hannah Darling, daughter of Pelatiah Darling and Elizabeth, wife, born Dec. 7, 1750.

Elizabeth Darling, daughter of Pelatiah Darling and Elizabeth, wife, born Feb. 8, 1753.

Abigail Darling, daughter of Pelatiah Darling and Elizabeth, wife, born April 15, 1755.

Joshua Darling, son of Pelatiah Darling and Elizabeth, wife, born August 19, 1762.

Pelatiah Darling, son of Pelatiah Darling and Elizabeth, wife, born April 2, 1760.

Ruth Darling, daughter of Pelatiah Darling and Elizabeth, wife, born June 5, 1766.

Rachael Darling, daughter of Pelatiah and Elizabeth, wife, born March 14, 1758.

Phinehas Darling, son of Pelatiah Darling and Elizabeth, wife, born March 20, 1769.

Luke Darling, daughter of Nathan Darling and Polly, wife, born June 18, 1794.

Nathan Darling, son of Nathan Darling and Polly, wife, born Jan. 12, 1796.

Cortis Darling, son of Nathan Darling and Polly, wife, born Dec. 30, 1797.

George Darling, son of Nathan Darling and Polly, wife, born Jan. 29, 1800.

Mehitable Darling, daughter of Samuel Darling and Sarah, his wife, born Sept. 7, 1746.

Caleb Darling, son of Samuel Darling and Sarah, his wife, born Nov. 30, 1748.

Deborah Darling, daughter of Samuel Darling, and Sarah, his wife, born July 6, 1750.

Peter Darling, son of Samuel Darling and Sarah, his wife, born June 20, 1752.

Trial Darling, daughter of Samuel Darling and Sarah, his wife, born May 20, 1754.

Aaron Darling, son of Samuel Darling and Sarah, his wife, born June 20, 1756.

Dinnis Darling, son of Samuel Darling and Sarah, his wife, born Feb. 20, 1760.

Henry Darling, son of Samuel Darling and Sarah, his wife, born July 3, 1762.

Patience Darling, daughter of Daniel Darling and Hannah, his wife, born Oct. 30, 1799.

Lovice Darling (twin), daughter of Daniel Darling and Hannah, his wife, born July 6, 1801.

Lucretia Darling (twin), daughter of Daniel Darling and Hannah, his wife, born July 6, 1801.

Gilson Darling, son of Daniel Darling and Hannah, his wife, born August 23, 1802.

James Darling, son of Daniel Darling and Hannah, his wife, born Feb. 10, 1804.

Elias Darling, son of Daniel Darling, and Hannah, his wife, born July 14, 1806.

Miranda Darling, daughter of Daniel Darling and Hannah, his wife, born July 19, 1808.

Clarissa Darling, daughter of Daniel Darling and Hannah, his wife, born May 30, 1810.

Eliza Ann Darling, daughter of Daniel Darling and Hannah, his wife, born June 12, 1812.

Sarah Darling, daughter of Daniel Darling and Hannah, his wife, born Aug. 28, 1815.

Daniel Darling, son of Daniel Darling and Hannah, his wife, born Oct. 19, 1817.

Ezekiel Emerson Darling, son of Daniel Darling and Hannah, his wife, born July 19, 1820.

Caleb Darling, son of Job Darling and Margery, his wife, born Sept. 5, 1768.

Mary Darling, dau. of Job Darling and Margery, his wife, born Dec. 23. 1769.

Hannah Darling, dau. of Job Darling and Margery, his wife, born Oct. 9, 1772.

John Darling, son of Leonard W. Darling and Relief, his wife, born Jan. 24, 1815.

Leonard Darling, son of Leonard W. Darling and Relief, his wife, born April 6, 1822.

Clarissa Darling, dau. of Leonard Darling and Relief, his wife, born Nov. 25, 1823.

John Darling, son of Phinehas Darling and Bethiah Kimton, born March 23, 1797.

Otis Darling, son of Phinehas Darling and Mary, his wife, born Feb. 2, 1803.

Phinehas Darling, son of Phinehas Darling and Mary, his wife, born Dec. 15, 1805.

Elizabeth Darling, wife of John Darling, deceased April 3, 1687.

Anna Darling, wife of John Darling, died April 30, 1690.

Denice Darling, deceased Jan. 25, 1717–18, aged 77 years.

Cortis Darling, son of Nathan Darling and Polly, his wife, died June 6, 1799.

Nathan Darling, son of Nathan Darling and Polly, his wife, died June 10, ——.

Seth Darling, son of John Darling, Jr. and Elizabeth, his wife, died Oct. 30, 1798.

Pardon Darling, son of John Darling, Jr., and Elizabeth, his wife, died Oct. 20, 1799.

Olive Darling, dau. of Mathew Darling and Hannah, his wife, died May 20, 1772.

Bethany Darling, dau. of Mathew Darling and Hannah, his wife, died March 17, 1777.

Phebe Darling, dau. of Mathew Darling and Hannah, his wife, died March 9, 1777.

Lovice Darling (twin), dau. of Daniel Darling and Hannah, his wife, died July 10, 1801.

Lucretia Darling (twin), dau. of Daniel Darling and Hannah, his wife, died July 11, 1801.

Miranda Darling, dau. of Daniel Darling and Hannah, his wife, died Dec. 25, 1826.

Elathan Darling, child of Jesse Darling and Hannah, his wife, died Aug. 6, 1793.

James Darling, son of Jesse Darling and Hannah, his wife, died May 6, 1804.

John Darling, died Oct. 29, 1800.

Jesse Darling, died July 9, 1813.

Lewis Darling, son of John Darling, died Aug. 20, 1818.

DARLINGS OF FRAMINGHAM, MASS.

Darling, John, and wife Abigail, lived in the north part of the town and had: 1, Abigail, b. June 2, 1736; 2, John, March 24, '37–8; 3, Amos, March 13, '43; 4, Timothy, Aug. 12, '47. Abigail, the wife, admitted to the church Feb. 5, 1748. (Sarah, of Framingham, m. Isaac Wheeler, of Holden, Aug. 18, 1752; John, son of Samuel, baptized June 18, 1758; Thomas, rated in Framingham, about 1738).

2. Amos, m. Hephzibah Bruce, in Southbridge, May 9, 1745, and, with wife, came in Framingham Nov., 17, '48; and had in Framingham, 1, Joseph, b. Oct. 29, 1746; 2, Elizabeth, b. March 2, '48, m. Eleazar Rice, of Marlboro, 1772; 3, Jonas, b. June 4 '53, m. Molly Knights and died in Sterling; 4, Lucy, b. Aug. 13 '55, m. Daniel Rice, of Marlboro; 5, Amos, b. June 16, '57, m. Laovisie Hager, of Marlboro; 6, Hephzibah, b. Dec. 8, '59, m. Levi Wilkins, of Marlboro, d. 1840; 7, Lydia, b. July 10, '62, d. unmarried, '89; 8, Daniel, b. July 24, '65, m. Rebeckah Arnold, of Marlboro, and 2d, Charlotte Hunting, lived in Marlboro, and d. in Framingham, 1844. Amos was recommended to the church in Marlboro, Aug., 1788, about which time his farm was set off to Marlboro. (Jacob, son of Amos, was baptized in Framingham, Nov. 27, 1748.)

3. Timothy, son of John (1), and wife, had: Timothy, baptized Oct. 28, 1770; 2, Nabby, baptized Nov. 25, 1770.

4. Joseph, son of Amos (2) m. Eunice Flagg, in Marlboro, 1773, and had: 1, Molly, b. May 8, 1774. The father m. 2d Sarah Houghton, and had: 2, John, b. April 1, 1781. Joseph lived in Framingham with Amos his father, and moved to Brattleboro, about 1781.

5. Margery, widow of Job, d. in Framingham, June of 1819, aged 85. Job d. in Framingham, March 26, 1814, aged 87.

Barry in his History of Framingham says: The tradition of the family relates that Amos Darling came from Danvers and that his grandfather came from England, when there were only fourteen houses in Salem. Thomas, only son of John, who d. 1713, and wife Joana were of Salem, 1690.

Daniel (w. Lydia) d. in Mendon about 1746, f. of Daniel, Samuel, Peter, William, and four daughters. Timothy was of Lunenburg, 1753. Benjamin of Wrentham (who had brothers John, Elias), died before the Revolution, an aged man, and was father of Rev. David of Surrey, N. H., who died 1836, aged 81. Judge Joshua, of Henniker, N. H., was probably a relative of this last. (See Wm. Barry's Hist. of Framingham, 1847.)

Ebenezer Darling and John Darling of Framingham were of Captain Newell's company in the Crown Point expedition, during the last French and Indian War, March 27, 1755, and were discharged January 3, 1756.

Amos Darling was the son of Ebenezer Darling, b. Jan. 8, 1679. Ebenezer, the father of Amos, was the son of Denice Darling, who died in Mendon, Mass., Jan. 25, 1717, aged 77 years, thus making his birth date 1640. It would seem that when Denice Darling, the grandfather, came from England (not earlier, of course, than 1640), there were more than fourteen houses in Salem. This record of the tradition given by Barry serves to show how little reliance should be placed on traditions when it is possible by researches to find actual data.

In the records of the Probate Office at East Cambridge I found the will of Thomas Darling of Framingham. His wife Sarah is named; his son John Darling is named, whom he gives five shillings, having before given him by a deed of gift——, which seems to have been his full share. The heirs of his son Jonathan Darling, deceased are named. Thomas Darling had a daughter, Sarah Darling, named in the will. The remainder of his estate went to his two sons, Ebenezer and Amos. The will is dated Sept. 8, 1749. In the same office there is the will of Ebenezer Darling of Framingham, and also an inventory of the estate. It is mentioned as in the Province of the Massachusetts Bay, and the order bears the date, 29 March, A. D. 1756. Amos Darling, on the 29th day of March, 1756, was admitted as the administrator.

An inventory April 15, 1756, " of the estate of Ebenezer Darling, late of Framingham, Dyst., seized and possessed of, is as followethe, viz.: the land estate of ye Ebenezer, of the homestead being about 140 acres, the one half being ye s^d Ebenezer, both of land and buildings which were appraised at four hundred and twenty-five pounds and ten shillings." Other small sums are mentioned.

The will of Job Darling of Framingham was admitted to Probate, 8 April, 1814. "Margery" Darling "my true and beloved wife" is named. His son Caleb Darling a "non compos " is also named. His daughter, Huldah Meriam, and her husband Timothy Meriam, are mentioned and are the last heirs; the sum of 50 dollars in cash is spoken of.

William Darling, a laborer of Charlestown, died intestate. This is mentioned in the probate office, under the date of 1746.

Sara, daughter of Xpper (Christopher) Darling, was christened March 13, 1624 at St. James, Clerkenwell, London.

There is, according to the English Pedigrees, a Darley of Yorkshire; the manuscripts are 234, 251.

There are old manuscripts containing pedigrees of the Darlings of London, Cornwall and Derbyshire.

Members of these families emigrated to America during the early settlement of the country.

ARMS OF GREY.

The arms here given may be deciphered as follows.

Barry of six argent and azure. Crest: A peacock's head and neck, between two wings erect, the feathers azure, and their pens (quills) argent. This crest of Sir Richard de Grey, K. G., 1420, A. D., is from the Garter Plate at Windsor; the crest rises from such a crest-coronet as was borne on the helms by noblemen in the time of Henry V.

Other immediate branches of these ancient Grey families bore for arms, barry of six argent and azure, in chief three torteaux. Another great branch of this ancient house of Grey, as will be seen in the following pages, adopted different armorial bearings, viz. : gules, a lion rampant with a bordure engrailed argent.

GRAY GENEALOGY.

Edward Gray, to whom reference has been made, came to Plymouth, Mass., with his brother Thomas Gray in 1643. Thomas Gray was the older of the two. He died at Plymouth, June 7, 1654.

Edward Gray was then a mere youth, and according to a tradition of the family, the two brothers were smuggled on board the ship in which they came, and were sent to America by friends at home who had been intriguing for the possession of the property which rightfully belonged to them. The oldest stone on Burial Hill is that of Edward Gray, on which is the following inscription: " Here lyeth ye body of Edward Gray, Gent, aged about 52 years,* and departed this life ye last of June, 1681." This stone of Edward Gray " is roughly made of a common shaky blue native slate, rudely cut and carved, and considering its material, it has surprisingly survived the ravages of time." " A strip of land running on Main street from Leyden to Middle street was once owned by Stephen Hopkins, one of the Mayflower Pilgrims. He died in 1644, and not long after his death it came into the hands of Edward Gray, who sold it in 1670 to John Cotton, then pastor of the Plymouth Church."

Robert Hicks was a leather dresser in London, and is supposed to have been a brother of Sir Baptist Hicks, a mercer of London, who was knighted in 1605, and afterwards became Viscount of Camden. He was the founder of Hicks' Hall, a Session House built in 1612, and made famous by the trial of Lord Russell† who was condemned within its walls, and of Count Königsmark, the

---

* Edward Gray at the time of his death, instead of being 52, as recorded on the gravestone at Plymouth, was upwards of 58 years of age, for the record of his baptism in Stapleford Tawney, Eng., is April 15, 1623.

† The condemnation of William Lord Russell was not, in fact, at Hicks's Hall, but at the Old Bailey, as is represented by a painting of the trial scene, made at that time. A reproduction of that painting is now in the possession of the author.

assassin of Mr. Thyme. Butler in the third canto of the third part of "Hudibras" alludes to it in the following lines:

> " One old dull sot who tol'd the clock
> For many years at Bridewell dock
> At Westminister's and Hicks's Hall,
> And Hiccius doctius played in all."

Robert Hicks conveyed the estate under consideration in 1639, to his son Samuel, and after the removal of Samuel to Barnstable and Dartmouth, it passed into the hands of Edward Gray, who made it his residence. In 1673, Edward Gray conveyed it to John Richard. This was a tract of land between Middle and Leyden streets, on the north and south, and Coles's Hill and Le Baron Alley, on the east and west. This covers two original garden plots, which as far back as the earliest records of Plymouth, belonged to Robert Hicks, who built a house there, which he made his residence. The lot of land on which the Plymouth Rock House now stands, at the conner of North Street and Coles's Hill, was a part of the land granted to James Cole, one of the early settlers referred to. Before 1685, it came into the possession of Nathaniel Clarke, who before the year 1700 seems to have been largely interested in land on that street. In 1697 he conveyed it to John Cole, and his wife Susannah Cole, who was the daughter of Dorothy, the wife of Mr. Clarke by her first husband, Edward Gray. In 1725 Susannah Cole, then a widow, conveyed it to Consider Howland, and the next year Mr. Howland conveyed it to John Foster, who sold it in 1734, to his brother Thomas Foster. In 1639, Robert Hicks sold a lot to his son Samuel Hicks, and when Samuel removed to the Cape, it passed into the hands of Edward Gray. In 1673, Mr. Gray sold it to John Richard already referred to, and it remained the property of Mr. Richard, and his son John until 1738, when it was sold by the latter to the second James Warren. In the same year Mr. Warren sold it to Lazarus Le Baron, who held it as a vacant lot until 1775, when in the division of his estate, that part which belongs to the Samoset House was set off to his son William, and the remainder, including Cushman Street and all the lots on both sides of it, to his son Isaac. The following is the property referred to : "Stephen Dean sold to Robert Hixe two acres of land lying on the north side of the town between the first and the second brooks, the one being his own inheritance, ye other was that he bought of Philip De Lelanoy, the which two acres he sold as aforesaid to the said Robert Hixe for the sum of four pounds sterling, which payment he hath received, and in witness hereof he hath put his hand, this 3d of July, 1630. Signed Stephen Dean." (From the Ancient Landmarks of Plymouth by William T. Davis.)

"Thomas Clarke, whose stone was placed on Burial Hill in 1697, has erroneously been thought to have been the mate of the Mayflower." He came to Plymouth in the "Anne" in 1623, and though in conflict with the inscription on his stone, he made oath in 1664, in an instrument signed by him, that he was fifty-nine years of age. This would have made him born in 1605, and in 1620 only fifteen years old, altogether too young for the position of mate. Nathaniel Clarke, whose grave-stone bearing the date of 1717 stood near that of his father, Thomas Clarke, was secretary of the Colony after the death of Nathaniel Morton in 1685. On the arrival of Andros as Governor of New England, he became one of the royal Governor's most willing and offensive tools. The title of Clark's Island, of which Plymouth in its municipal capacity had held undisputed possession since 1638, when all lands within its limits not included in previous allotments were granted by the court to the town, was, with other titles, proclaimed as vested in the King. Clarke, who was a member of the Council, applied for a grant of the Island, and finally obtained it against remonstrance and resistance of the inhabitants of the town. The original instrument making the grant is now in existence. At this juncture news was received from the mother country of the revolution of 1688, and Andros and Clarke were arrested and sent to England. After his release by the King, Clarke returned to Plymouth, and continued there in the practice of the law until his death. Nathaniel Clarke married Dorothy, daughter of Thomas and Ann Lettice and widow of Edward Gray above mentioned. They became owners of the whole square, including the upper and lower lots, which were already the property of Mr. Clarke. They had other large property (op. citata.)

Dr. James Thatcher in his history of Plymouth says: "No stone of an earlier date than 1681 is to be found on Burial Hill of Plymouth, though it is by no means probable that this was the first interment here." It is to the memory of Edward Gray, a respectable merchant, whose name frequently occurs in the old records of Plymouth. He made his mark for his name, as was not uncommon in those days. By habits of industry and good management, he gained the character of a respectable merchant, and acquired an estate worth £1250 sterling, the largest estate at that time in the colony.

The second Edward, according to accounts, received from Lewis Bradford, Esq., certain estates which were at Tiverton, R.I.

Thomas and Samuel lived at Little Compton, R. I.

William Bradford was born at Austerfield, in the county of York, England; he was baptised March, 1589. He married for his first wife Dorothy Hay, by whom he had one son whose name was John. There is no account that this John was ever married; there is a tradition that he was lost at sea on his passage to England. The maiden name of the Governor's second wife, Mrs. Southworth, widow of Constant Southworth, was Alice Carpenter. By this union he had three children, viz.: William, Mercy, and Joseph.

It deserves to be stated that the father of William Bradford, the emigrant ancestor, whose name was William Bradford, died in 1591, when his son was only two years old.

Mercy[2] Bradford m. Benjamin Vermegue.

William Bradford son of Governor Bradford and Mrs. Alice Southworth Bradford, his wife, obtained high distinction in the colony. He was elected assistant soon after the death of his father and was chosen military commander. He had the title of major; he was an active officer in King Philip's war. He married for his first wife Alice Richards. The date of his birth being June 17, 1624. She died in 1671, aged 44 years. By her he had four sons, viz.: John, William, Thomas and Samuel. When the colonial government terminated in 1692, Major Bradford was deputy governor and afterward was chosen counsellor of Massachusetts. He died 20th Feb., 1703, aged 79 years.

John, the oldest son of William Bradford and Alice Richards Bradford, his wife, was born Feb., 1653. He is frequently mentioned in the Plymouth records as a selectman; he served on various committees; in 1692 was deputy. He was representative to the General Court.

Major John Bradford married Mercy Warren, daughter of Joseph Warren. The children were: John, Alice, Abigail, Mercy, Samuel, Priscilla, and William. He died Dec. 8, 1736, in his 84th year. Mercy, his widow, died in 1747, in her 94th year.

The Governor's son Joseph lived near Jones' River. Joseph had a son Elisha, who had several children.

Lieutenant Samuel Bradford, son of Major John Bradford, married Sarah Gray, daughter of Edward Gray, of Tiverton, R. I., and granddaughter of Edward Gray of Plymouth. The issue was John, Gideon, and William, who died young, Mary, and Sarah, William and Mercy, who also died young, Abigail, Phebe and Samuel. Lieutenant Samual Bradford lived in Plymouth. He died there in 1740, aged 56 years.

The Hon. William Bradford, late of Bristol, R. I., was son of the above Samuel Bradford. He was born at Plympton, Mass., Nov. 4, 1729. He died July, 1808. He was Deputy Governor of Rhode Island, Speaker of the House of Representatives, and member of Congress. He lived near Mount Hope, celebrated as having been the residence of the famous King Philip, the aboriginal proprietor. His descendants were numerous.

Daniel Bradford was probably a son of William Bradford. Le Baron Bradford was a younger son of William. Polly Bradford, daughter of William, married Henry Goodwin of Boston, May 20, 1782.

From the history of James Thatcher, M.D., A.A.S., 1835, the following is the summary: —

Governor William Bradford, born 1590; first wife Dorothy Hay; had son John Bradford; but there is no further record. The Governor's second wife was Mrs. Southworth; her maiden name was Alice Carpenter. Their children were: William, Mercy, and Joseph. William, the Governor's son, was major in King Philip's War. His wife was Mrs. Alice Richards. Their four sons were : John, William, Thomas and Samuel. John, the oldest son of Major Bradford, was deputy; John was also major. He married Mercy Warren, daughter of Joseph Warren. The children were: John, Alice, Abigail, Mercy, Samuel, Priscilla, and William. Samuel, son of John, was Lieutenant. Lieutenant Bradford married Sarah Gray, born April 25, 1697, daughter of Edward Gray, of Tiverton, and granddaughter of Edward Gray, of Plymouth. Lieutenant Samuel Bradford had a son William, who was the Hon. William Bradford. Hon. William Bradford was Deputy Governor of Rhode Island. He lived in Bristol, R. I., near Mount Hope, celebrated as having been the residence of the famous King Philip. His descendants were numerous.

The following is substantially from John Osborn Austin's Genealogical Dictonary of the first settlers of Rhode Island :

"Edward Gray m. 1651, Jan. 16, Mary Winslow, b. 1630, daughter of John and Mary (Chilton) Winslow; she died 1663. Edward m. (2) 1665, Dec. 12, Dorothy Lettice, b. 1648, daughter of Thomas and Ann Lettice; she m. (2) Nathaniel Clarke, born 1643 ; she died 1728 ; Edward Gray died 1681.

Nathaniel Clarke, her second husband died —1717 (according to the inscription on the gravestone).

Edward Gray was a merchant and was at Plymouth in 1643. (He was baptized April 15, 1623, as before stated.)

1650—Aug. 7. Edward Gray was to have a bushel of Indian corn for damage done by the cattle of Edward Doty in his corn.

1655—May 1. He was complained of by Samuel Cuthbert regarding a cow exchanged by Gray for a lot. The court found Cuthbert's complaint in a great measure unjust, Gray having, as appeared, given Cuthbert leave to make choice of a cow out of his cattle, whereupon the court persuaded Gray to accept three bushels of Indian corn for wintering the cow, and so the defense ended.

1656—Feb. 3. He having had a controversy with Francis Billington about two iron wedges, the court ordered them to be delivered to the latter.

1658—Feb. 2. He complained against Joseph Billington for neglecting to pay a small debt due.

1659—Dec. 6. He and another appeared at court to lay claim

to a parcel of iron wedges, which an Indian had stolen, and sold at Taunton, and the court took a course to have the Indian apprehended.

1662—June 3.   He was granted a double share of land.

1662—June 10.   The house bought by the country of him was to be repaired by order of the court.

1666—Oct. 31.   He was awarded 20s. from Joseph Billington for hunting his ox with a dog and for wrong done his swine and fence, and he was to have returned to him the scythes used by Billington without Gray's leave.

1667—March 5.   His land at Rocky Nook, Plymouth, was to be ranged and to have a highway laid out by it.

1668—June 3.   He was fined ten shillings for using reviling speeches to John Bryant, on the Lord's day, as soon as he came out of the meeting.

1668—Oct. 29.   He was to have two barrels of tar returned him, and eight shillings paid him for proving it was his.

1669—March 2.   John Bryant was fined 10 shillings for using reviling speeches to Edward Gray as soon as they came out of meeting, on the Lord's day.

1670—May 29.   Freeman.

1670—June 24.   He and seven others agreed for two years to pay 8 shillings per small barrel, and 12 shillings per great barrel, for good merchantable tar delivered at Waterside in good casks.

" June 10, 1670.   Tuspaquin, and his son William, sold for £6, to *Edward Gray*, in the behalf of the Court of Plimouth all that our meddow that lyeth in or neare the town of Middlebury, on the west side of a tract belonging to John *Alden* and *Constant Southworth*, and is between Assowamsett Pond, and Taunton Path, being in three parcels upon three brookes; also another parcel on the other side of Taunton path. Witnessed by *Amie*, the wife of *Tuspaquin* and two English. "

" 30 June, 1672—Tuspaquin, Sachem of Namassakett and Mantowapuct, alias *William*, his son. "

"Sell to *Edward Gray* and Josias *Winslow* lands on the easterly side of Assowamsett, to begin where Namasket River falleth out of the pond, and so south by the pond; thence by perishable bounds to Tuspaquin's Pond and so home to the lands formerly sold to *Henry Wood.*" (See Drake's Indian book III., pp. 53-54.)

1671—March 8. He was to have paid him 20 shillings from a man for pilfering his tobacco, and the culprit was whipped at the post and ordered to depart the government.

1671—Grand Jury.

1674—March 4. He was granted 100 acres at Titicut.

1676—77-78-79-Deputy.

1677—July 13. He was on committee respecting debts due the colony, and to balance accounts between towns concerning the late war.

1677—Oct. 3. He was to have, with two others, all the herbage and grass which shall grow on the country's lands at Pocassett and places adjoining, for one year, they paying £10 for the privilege.

1678—June 6. He was licensed to sell some small quantities of liquor as he may have occasion, to such as are or may be employed by him in fishing, and such like occasion, for their use and refreshing.

1680—March 5. He and seven others bought Pocasset (Tiverton) lands for £1,100 of Gov. Josiah Winslow. His share was 9-30 of the purchase.

1681—July 7. Administration to widow Dorothy.

1683—March 8. The court allowed his widow £60 out of his estate towards bringing up his three youngest children.

1684—July 1. She was granted £30 for her charges and trouble as administratrix. Guardians were chosen by her children this year as follows: Edward and Hannah chose Captain Nathaniel Thomas; Thomas, Rebecca, Lydia and Samuel chose Captain Nathaniel Thomas and their mother Dorothy Gray; Anna chose John Walley.

1684—Oct. 28. Mrs. Dorothy Gray consented that her husband's lands should be divided amongst his children before her dower was set off. She brought in her account showing inventory of £1,230, 12s., 11d., balanced by debts paid, and £67, 15s. 10d. divided to widow and children by order of the court.

Among items of inventory were money, plate goods and chattels, £737, 2s. 6d.; debts certain, uncertain and desperate, £346, 18s. 3d. Ketch at sea sold for £40, etc. Among the payments was allowance to widow " for long and great trouble in her said office by making up accounts with many persons, both debtors and creditors, at home and at Boston ; receiving from and paying debts to many several persons, and charge to others I employed to write and keep accounts clear ; and while I was busied every day about the concerns of the estate in general I was fain to hire a nurse for my younger child, which cost me for about four or five months time three shilling per week, and her diet which came to five or six pounds; and it is about three years' time that I have been thus concerned about the estate in general, with neglect to my own particular concerns, and judge I may well deserve at least fifty pounds, whereof the court allows thirty pounds.

1686—July 10. "Dorothy Clarke complains against her husband Nathaniel in order to a divorce, and there being such an uncomfortable difference between said Clarke and his wife, fearing lest they should ruin each other in their estate, have mutually agreed to a settlement until the law otherwise determines. The new house is in Nathaniel Clarke's possession as his and his wife's estate, she having liberty to live in part of said house to quantity of half if she pleases.

" Clarke to have all estate he brought with him, and she to have all estate she brought with her except what she had disposed of. Clarke to have one hogshead of rum in his hands for the finishing of the new house, and three barrels of cider for his own drinking, or at his dispose. She to deliver to him bond given her before marriage and he not to be liable for her debts, nor for administration by her on estate of her late husband Edward Gray ; Dorothy not to be charged with Clarke's contracts, etc."

Nathaniel Clarke referred to was the youngest son of Thomas Clarke known as counsellor Clarke.

Thatcher, one of the earliest historians of Plymouth, who was brought up among the descendants of the Pilgrims, says of Thomas Clarke :

" It is a well received tradition that this ancient man was the mate of the Mayflower and the one who first landed on the Island which bears his name. It may be conjectured that he was considered merely an officer of the ship, and that he returned to England in her, with Captain Jones, and subsequently came over and settled in this town." (History of Plymouth). Nathaniel Clarke, of Plymouth, was born 1643; he was educated in the law office of Secretary Morton, and was known as councellor Clarke. His house was on the Main street; the same house afterwards occupied by Judge Thomas. Andros made a grant of Clarke's Island, which the people refused to confirm, and he failed of securing the property. He married Dorothy Lettice Gray, widow of Edward Gray, a rich merchant of Plymouth, but they did not live together comfortably, and after much scandal she left him, but afterwards, says Thatcher, returned to live with him. He died without issue Jan. 31, 1717, aged 74; she died in 1728, aged 80 years. (Records of some of the descendants of Thomas Clarke, of Plymouth, 1623).

The children of Edward Gray and Mary (Winslow) Gray, his wife, were:

1. Desire, b. Nov. 6, 1651, m. 1672, Jan. 10, Nathaniel Southworth, b. 1648, son of Constant and Elizabeth Southworth. She died 1690, Dec. 4. He died 1711, Jan. 14.

2. Mary, b. 1653, Sept. 18.

3. Elizabeth, b. 1658, Feb. 11.

4. Sarah, b. 1659, August 12.

5. John, b. 1661, Oct. 1, married Joanna Morton.

The children of Edward Gray by his second wife, Dorothy (Lettice), were:

6. Edward, b. 1667, Jan. 31, Tiverton, R. I., m. (1) Mary Smith, daughter of Philip and Mary Smith; m. (2) Mary Manchester, daughter of William and Mary (Cook) Manchester.

1696 Oct. 7. He bought certain land in Tiverton, of Caleb and Lydia Loring of Plymouth for £230. He died 1726. His wife Mary (Manchester) d. 1729.

1722 Dec. 10. "Will proved 1726, June 7. Executors, sons Philip and Thomas. To wife Mary, while widow, the new addition on east side house and use of six rows apple trees, and liberty to cut wood, improvement of garden, £100, 6 best cows, 1 mare, negro woman Zilpha and 1-4 household stuff.

" To son Philip,3 fifty-acre lots where I live, buildings, orchard, etc., and other land, he paying my son Thomas £20, and to daughter Hannah, 1 feather bed, etc., to value of £150. To son Thomas, 3 fifty-acre lots, etc., he paying my daughter Sarah legacy with what she has to make her up to £130. To sons Philip and Thomas, jointly, land where my son Edward formerly lived, with buildings, etc., they paying my daughter Elizabeth so much as shall make up what I gave her in life time, which appears by book £150, and also paying bonds which testator obliges himself to pay to daughter-in-law Rebecca Gray, to pay to children of my son Edward, deceased. To son John, 27 acres &c., he paying legacy to my daughter Lydia Gray, of £120, good feather bed, &c. To son William under age, 120 acres &c., £20, and negro Sambo. To son Samuel, 60 acres and £250 when 21. To sons William and Samuel, land. To daughter Mary, wife of John Bennet, 5s, she having had her part. To daughter Phebe £150. If either son had by 1st wife, die before 21, his part to go to surviving son of 1st wife. If either of sons of last wife die without issue, then part to go to surviving son of last wife. All estate not disposed of to go equally to eight youngest children, viz.: Philip, Thomas, John, William, Samuel, Phebe, Hannah, and Lydia.

1729—March 19. Inventory, £284, 9s. 10d. Widow Mary. Administration to brother John Manchester."

7. Susanna, b. 1668, Oct. 15.

8. Thomas, b. 1670, settled in Little Compton, R. I., m. (1) Anna, b. 1673, d. 1706, Oct. 16; m. (2) Phebe, daughter of John Peckham, b. 1666, d. 1746.

1704—Nov. 1. Thomas Gray and William Pabodie signed a letter on behalf of the Congregational Church inviting neighboring churches to the ordination of Rev. Richard Billings, which was to take place Nov. 29.

1721—Sept. 21. "Will proved 1721, Nov. 23, executors, sons Thomas and Edward. To wife Phebe, looking-glass, brass kettle, new bible, plate, cup, two silver spoons, warming-pan, two feather beds, negro maid Peg and one-half household stuff, also great room, bedroom, cheese room and cellar in house called ' Woodworth's house,' while widow, and to have ten cords of wood per year, ten bushels Indian corn, barley, meat, etc., two cows, and keep of same, the new garden and £8 per year. To son Thomas, dwelling house and fifty acre lot, and other land. To son Edward, dwelling house he now liveth in, fifty acres, and other land. To daughter Anna Richmond, mulatto girl 'Almy,' gold ring, silver spoon and bible. To daughter Rebecca Gray, two feather beds, one half of household stuff, one gold ring, one silver spoon and £50 and 3 cows. To sons Thomas and Edward, each a feather bed, and son Thomas a clock, gun, silver spoon, gold ring, negro called 'Sarah' mulatto boy 'Solomon' and five cows. To son Edward, book called Josephus, gold ring, silver spoon, negro called 'Will' (letting him have one day a month to himself), mulatto boy called 'Jeffrey,' and five cows. To three grandchildren, Barzilla Richmond, Mary Gray and Anstis Gray, one cow each. To daughter Rebecca, a good suit of apparel and house room till better provided for. To kinsman Nathaniel Gibbs, son of Warren Gibbs, three sheep and three lambs. To two sons equally, land in Plymouth, Tiverton, etc., and rest of movables."

"Inventory: dwelling house and 50 acres, £800; Dwelling house and 50 acres where Edward lives, £800; other lots of land, £1000, £540, £500, £250, etc.; 6 working cattle, 19 cows, 6 two-year cattle, 14 yearlings, 4 fat oxen, 14 calves, 3 mares, 3 colts, 4 two-year horses, 2 yearling mares, 6 score sheep, 4 score lambs, swine; negro, £30; negro woman, £30; mulatto boy, £50; mulatto boy, £45; 2 mulatto girls, £50 each; 1 silver cup, 6 silver spoons, malt mill, 2 cheese presses, 4 tables, 15 leather chairs, 15 other chairs, case with 9 bottles, 13 pewter platters, 33 pewter plates, 11 porringers, 7 candlesticks, 1 warming pan, 1 gun, etc.

"1723—July 8. Will, proved 1723, August 7, of his son Thomas; mentions honored mother-in-law (i. e., stepmother), Phebe Gray, brother of Edward Gray; brother-in-law, William Richmond and sister Anna his wife; sister Rebecca, wife of John Pabodie, etc.

"1746—May 16. Will, proved 1746, Dec. 15, widow Phebe, aged 80, late of Little Compton, now of Middletown, R. I. Ex., cousin John Taylor, of Middletown. To cousin John Taylor, all estate.

9. " Samuel, born ——, married 1699, July 13, Deborah Church born 1672, daughter of Joseph and Mary (Tucker) Church. He died 1712, March 23. She married (2) Daniel Throope.

"1712—March 20. Will, proved 1712, April 7; executors, wife and brother, Thomas Gray. Overseers, friend William Pabodie, Captain John Palmer and brother John Church. To wife Deborah, improvement of whole estate for children's maintenance while widow. If she marry, to have £100. At marriage or decease of wife, all estate to be divided as follows : To eldest son Samuel, £300. To sons, Simeon and Ignatius, £100 each. To daughters Dorothy and Lydia, £100 each. If the estate proves worth more than £800, the residue to go to two youngest sons, Simeon and Ignatius. Inventory £1,138 9s. 7d., viz.: farm and buildings, orchard, etc., £850, outlands £26, feather beds, pewter, 1 pair of worsted combs, 3 pair of old cards, 1 wooden wheel, 2 common wheels, 1 churn, 1 cradle, 1 cheese press, 1 warming pan, silver money £12 4s. 7d., 3 mares, 14 cows, 1 heifer, 5 two-year old, 3 yearlings, 5 calves, 1 pair oxen, etc.

"1713—June 3. Deborah Throope, wife of Daniel Throope, of Bristol, late wife of Samuel Gray, of Little Compton, gave receipt to Thomas Gray.

10. " Hannah. b. ——, d.——.

11. " Rebecca, b. ——, d. ——, m. Ephraim Cole, son of James Cole.

12. " Lydia, m. 1696, Aug. 7, Caleb Loring, b. 1674, June 9, son of Thomas and Hannah (Jacob) Loring of Plympton, Mass., from whom the Lorings in the north part of that town had descended."

13. Anna, b. ——, d. ——.

The children of Desire Gray, who m. Nathaniel Southworth, were :—

1. Constant, b. 1674, Aug. 12.
2. Mary, b. 1676, April 3.
3. Ichabod, b. 1678, March.
4. Nathaniel, b. 1684, May 10.
5. Elizabeth.
6. Edward, b. 1688.

The children of Samuel Gray and Deborah Church were : —
1. Samuel, b. 1700, April 16, d. April 22, 1764.
2. John, b. 1701, April 14; d. Jan. 14, 1702.
3. Dorothy, b. 1704, Jan. 14.
4. Joseph, b. 1706, Jan. 21.
5. Lydia, b. 1707, Oct. 16.
6. Simon, b. 1709, Dec. 15.
7. Ignatius, b. 1711, Sept. 18; d. July 18, 1712.

Children of Lydia Gray and Caleb Loring, her husband, were :—
1. Caleb, b. 1697, June 7.
2. Hannah, b. 1698, Aug. 7.
3. Ignatius, b. 1699, Dec. 27.
4. Polycarpus, b. 1702.
5. Caleb, b. 1704, Oct. 2.
6. Lydia, b. 1706.
7. Jacob, b. 1711, May 15.
8. Joseph, b. 1713, July 25.
9. John, b. 1715, Nov. 15.
10. Thomas, b. 1718, April 18.
11. Lydia, b. 1721, Aug 23.

The children of Rebecca Gray and her husband, Ephraim Cole, were : —

Ephraim, b. 1691; Samuel, b. 1694; Rebecca, 1696; Mary, 1698; Dorothy, 1701; James, 1705; Samuel, 1709.

The children of John Gray and Joanna Morton were: —

Edward, 1687; Mary, 1688; Ann, 1691; Desire, 1693; Joanna, 1696; Samuel, 1702; Mercy, 1704.

The children of Edward Gray and Mary Smith (1), his wife, were : —
1. Mary, b. 1691, May 16.
2. Edward, b. 1693, Jan. 10.
3. Elizabeth, b. 1695, Jan. 3.
4. Sarah, b. 1697, April 25.
5. Phebe, b. 1699, Sept. 6.
6. Philip, b. 1702, Feb. 11.
7. Thomas, b. 1704, Feb. 4.

8. Hannah, b. 1707, Nov. 3.
(2 wife, Mary Manchester).
9. John, b. 1712, August 3.
10. Lydia, b. 1714, May 12.
11. William, b. 1716, July 17.
12. Samuel, b. 1718, August 31.

The children of Thomas^2 Gray, (Edward^1) and Anna, his wife, were : —

1. Thomas, b. 1695, May 7.
2. Edward, b. 1699, Nov. 29.
3. Anna, b. 1702, Jan. 29.
4. Rebecca, 1704, August 1.
5. Mary, 1706, Oct. 8.

(2 wife, Phebe Peckham, without issue).

[The above extracts are from J. O. Austin's Gen. Dict., R. I., as aforesaid.]

Samuel^3 Gray (Samuel^2, Edward^1,) married 1721 (intention of marriage Dec. 17, 1720, in Bristol, R. I.), Hannah Kent of Barrington, R. I. (b. 1703, died July 1, 1796).

Their children were : —

Desire, b. Nov. 27, 1721 ; died Oct. 1, 1732.
Deborah, b. Oct.. 1, 1723 ; died March 7, 1726.
Samuel, b. May 12, 1726 ; died March 30, 1813.
Hannah, b. April 22, 1728; died Feb, 1, 1812.
Deborah, (2) b. Nov. 26, 1730.
Lydia, b. March 20, 1733.
Desire (2), July 7, 1735 ; d. March, 1822.
Mary, b. July 5, 1739.
Thomas, b. Sept. 7, 1741.
Simeon, b. Jan. 16, 1743.
Lois, b. June 12, 1745.

There was a Thomas Gray who was born in Little Compton, R. I., Sept., 7, 1741. He was son of Samuel, born 1700, April 16, and grandson of Samuel Gray, born 1682 and died March 23, 1712. (Thomas^4, Samuel^3, Samuel^2, Edward^1).

The first Samuel seems to have been ten years younger than his wife, but seventeen years old when married ; this is the record, however improbable. The first Samuel Gray also seems to have been born after the death of his father, the first Edward.

Samuel[4] Gray (Samuel[3], Samuel[2], Edward[1]), of Little Compton, married Oct, 25, 1750, Deborah Peck, of Bristol, R. I.

Their children were : —

Hannah Gray, b. Nov, 8, 1751 ; died in 1755.

Fallee, b. April 23, 1754.

John, b. March 20, 1756.

Simeon, b. April 15, 1758 ; d. 1781.

Lydia, b. Jan. 22, 1761.

Elizabeth, b. July 23, 1763.

Samuel, b. Sept. 29, 1765.

Thomas, b. April 22, 1767.

Jonathan, b. March 9, 1771.

Joshua, b. Nov. 10, 1773 ; d. 1775.

Nathaniel, b. March 20, 1776 ; d. 1836.

Loren and Benjamin (twins), b. Feb. 5, 1779.

Philip[3] Gray (Edward[2], Edward[1]), married Sarah, and the children were as follows : —

Philip, b. April 6, 1728.

Pardon, b. April 20, 1737.

Philip (2), b. June 22, 1750.

Pardon[4] Gray (Philip[3], Edward[2], Edward[1]), married Mary, and had the following : —

Job, b. May 14, 1756, m. Juliette Briggs of Tiverton, Dec. 16, 1781.

Sarah, b. May 3, 1758.

Edward, b. July 8, 1759, had daughter Elizabeth, who married William Briggs Oct. 15, 1778.

Mary, b. August 3, 1761.

Lydia, b. March 15, 1763.

Abigail, b. Aug. 2, 1764.

Philip, b. Feb. 2, 1766.

Pardon, b. Oct. 11, 1767.

Hannah, b. May 2, 1769.

John, b. May, 20, 1772.

Thomas, b. Nov. 28, 1774.

Mary, b. Nov. 18. 1776.

Thomas[3] Gray, born Feb. 4, 1704, son of Edward[2] (Edward[1]) married Elizabeth Sweet, March 21, 1722; m. (2) Sarah Bennet, Nov. 19, 1729. Notice of intention of marriage between Thomas Gray and Sarah Bennet, both of Tiverton, was entered October 28, 1728. The son of Thomas Gray and Elizabeth (Sweet) his wife was: Edward Gray,b. January 14, 1725.

The children of Thomas[3] Gray (Edward[2], Edward[1]), and Sarah (Bennet), his second wife, were :

Thomas Gray, b. Jan. 27, 1729.

Daniel, b. Oct. 14, 1731.

Mary, b. Oct. 14, 1733.

John, b. Sept. 19, 1736.

Elizabeth, b. Jan. 30, 1738-9.

Phebe, b. Nov. 17, 1740.

Sarah, b. March 17, 1742-3.

Gideon, b. Aug. 7, 1745.

Phebe Gray, widow of John Durfee, to whom she was married Dec. 15, 1757, died Feb. 12, 1819. The record says she was aged 79 years, 2 months, and 29 days.

Thomas, son of Pardon Gray, b. Nov. 28, 1774.

Thomas, son of Edward Gray, b. Nov. 25, 1756.

Thomas[4] Gray (Thomas[3], Edward[2], Edward[1]), son of Thomas[3] Gray and Sarah Bennet Gray, his wife, was born Jan. 27, 1729. He was married to Abigail Brown, born Feb. 21, 1731-2, daughter of Abraham Brown and Sarah his wife " in Tiverton in ye Colony of Rhode Island on ye fifth of November, A.D. 1747, by Samuel Durfee, justice apeace." Thomas Gray afterward settled in Bristol, R. I., where he bought of Nathaniel Munroe a large tract of the famous Mount Hope Lands. The purchase was made Jan. 17, 1769, in the ninth year of His Majesty's reign, and recorded January twenty-first, 1769, in Book no 3, page 220, of the Records of Land Evidence for said Bristol. According to the census return of Bristol in the year 1774, Thomas Gray was residing there at that time. His family consisted of one male above 16 years, three males under 16 years, two females above 16 years and two females under 16 years. Total in family eight persons.

Thomas Gray was illustrious in the service in the War of the Revolution. In 1775, both Houses of the Legislature of Rhode Island joined in the grand committees of the Army of Observation. Thomas Gray was commissioned as Captain, Silas Talbot as Lieutenant and Reuben Sprague as ensign, for the Ninth Company, to be raised in the counties of Newport and Bristol. Officers for the other companies, were also commissioned at this time.

These companies for the various counties, says the author of the "Spirit of Rhode Island in the War of the Revolution," soon filled up, and were on their march to join the grand army near Boston. Never, perhaps, had "His Majesty an army sooner enlisted and equipped for his service than this Army of Observation of Rhode Island in 1775. The blood of the martyrs at Lexington was as 'seed' which was soon scattered over the whole country, and it fell on 'good soil' in every part of the land, and by the blessings of God 'brought forth fruit abundantly.' A fire was kindled in the breasts of men that burnt up the 'tory stubble' in the colony, and was not extinguished until Great Britian herself acknowledged our independence, based upon the principle that whenever any form of government becomes destructive of its ends, it is the right of the people to alter or abolish it and to institute new government laying its foundation on such principles and organizing its powers in such form as to them shall seem most likely to effect their safety and supremacy."

1776.—Captain Thomas Gray was commissioned as Lieutenant Colonel of the First Regiment, Bristol County, R. I. Nathaniel Martin, Esq , was Colonel and Jesse Maxom, Esq., was Major.

Thomas Gray afterward was commissioned as Colonel and continued his service in the War of the Revolution.

The children of Thomas Gray and Abigail (Brown) Gray, his wife, were :—

1.   John Gray b. —— ; m. ——.
2.   Meribah, b. —— ; m. —— Shaw ; m. (2) —— Munroe.
3.   Ruth, b. —— ; m. Thomas Waldron, Feb. 1, 1778. He settled in the state of Pennsylvania.

The children of Ruth and Thomas Waldron, her husband, as given in rhyme of the old folk were :—

> "Steady Nat, Skinner John,
>   Kean Billings, Great Tom,
>   Pleasant Ambrose, Oh, dear Ben,
>   Nice Josie, Throupe and Sam,
>   Pretty Abbie and Becky. "

4.   Abigail, b. ——; m. ——Peck.

5.   Pardon, b. 1764 ; m. Reliance Davis, b. 1764.

Thomas Gray died in Tiverton 1803, while there after attending a funeral, according to one account, the funeral of his brother John ; according to another account, that of his son John. In his will, made Nov. 7, 1803, and proved Dec, 5, 1803, Thomas Gray declares that his son John was then deceased.

Mrs. Thomas (Abigail Brown) Gray died in Bristol, R. I. at the old homestead on Metacom Avenue. Both were buried in Tiverton, R. I.

The will made 1803, Nov. 7, was proved 1803, Dec. 5. To his wife Abigail all his household furniture and indoor movables ; also his negro woman " Hannah " and negro boy " Richard, " together with riding mare, woman's saddle, one cow such as she may choose from among his cows at the time of his decease. Also that his son Pardon furnish and provide for the aforesaid Abigail, yearly so long as she remain his widow, two hundred weight of good beef, and two hundred weight of pork, fifteen bushels of merchantable Indian corn, thirty weight of flax and twenty weight of wool, and to pay her twenty dollars yearly, so long as she remains his widow : his son Pardon to cut and draw to the door as much wood as may be necessary for her use. To have a privilege in the orchard for as much fruit, summer and winter, as she may need for her own consumption, and to be furnished with three barrels of cider yearly, provided the orchard affords as much. Also his wife Abigail to have the use and improvement of all the new part of his dwelling house situated in the Township of Bristol, with the garden to the northward, with the privilege of keeping any kind of poultry in and about the house and yard. Also that his son, Pardon Gray, furnish keeping, summer and winter, for the horse and cow so long as she remains his widow. He mentions in his will his son John, deceased, to whom he had deeded his share of the real estate to be distributed amongst his children and to his wife. He gives to John's children one dollar each. To his son Pardon, all his lands and buildings thereon situated in the Township of Bristol. To daughter, Meribah Munroe, one hundred and twenty dollars. To daughter, Ruth Waldron, one hundred and thirty dollars. To daughter, Abigail Peck, one hundred and twenty dollars. The remainder of his estate to his son Pardon, further to enable him to perform the duties enjoined upon him by his will. His son, Pardon Gray, was sole executor.

Pardon[5] Gray (Thomas[4], Thomas[3], Edward[2], Edward[1]), born in 1764; married Reliance Davis, born in 1764. Pardon Gray died in Bristol, R. I., August 16, 1826, in his 63d year. Mrs. Reliance (Davis) Gray died Nov. 9, 1838, in her 75th year. Their burial place is in Bristol. Their children were:

1. Elijah, b. ——; m. Lydia Jones; m. (2) Caroline Twiss, widow.

2. Thomas, b. ——; m. (1) ——, m. (2), —— Chase.

3. Lydia, b. ——; married —— Liscomb.

4. Ann Davis (called sometimes Nancy), b. ——; m. Aug. 31, 1817, Sylvanus Goff, their daughter Emily Goff, married Hon. John W. Davis, a prominent merchant, and Governor of Rhode Island.

5. Sarah, b. ——; married —— Liscomb.

6. John, b. ——; married Althea Meiggs, had several daughters, and son John, who studied for the ministry and was rector of a Reformed Episcopal Society.

7. Gideon, b. Oct. 10, 1804; married Dec. 3, 1826, Hannah (Metcalf) Orne, daughter of Joseph and his wife, Jane (Metcalf) Orne; Hannah b. Nov. 19, 1793. He died Dec. 13, 1871. His wife, Mrs. Hannah Gray, died Aug. 14, 1885.

8. Reliance, b. ——; married James Meiggs. Had several sons and daughters.

9. Mary Durfee, b. ——; died young.

The children of Gideon Gray and Hannah (Orne) Gray, his wife, were: —

1. William Bramwell, b. Dec. 12, 1827; m. Apr. 5, 1852, Martha Hale White, da. of Henry White and Betsy (Tibbets) White.

2. Gustavus Tucker, b. Sept. 7, 1830; married Jan. 2, 1853, Caroline Bourne Cooke, da. of Nicholas W. Cooke and Almy G. (Merrill) Cooke.

3. Eliza Jane, b. June 15, 1829, d. Aug. 21, 1842.
4. Charles Sidney, b. Oct., 1831-2, d. Oct. 18, 1833.
5. Mary Hannah Gray, b. Mar. 28, 1835; m. Oct. 23, 1861, Augustus Peck Clarke. She d. in Cambridge, Mass, May 30, 1892.
6. Louisa Bailey Gray, b. July 29, 1837; m. Aug. 27, 1857, Leonard Bradford⁹ Wright, son of Leonard and Nancy Bradford⁸ Wright. He was b. July 4, 1837. Louisa died April 14, 1881. Their children were :
1. Charles Sidney Wright, b. Dec. 9, 1858, died young.
2. Herbert Bradford Wright, b. Apr. 27, 1860.
3. Ellestein Louise Wright, b. May 8, 1862.
4. Winfield Elmer Wright, b. Apr. 23, 1864.
5. Jennie Gray Wright, b. May 12. 1866, died young.
6. Jennie Gray Wright, b. Sept. 3, 1867.
7. Leonard Smith Wright, b. Apr. 20, 1869, died young. And others also that died young.

Mrs. Nancy Bradford Wright, the mother of Leonard Bradford Wright, was a lineal descendant in the eighth generation in descent from William Bradford, the Mayflower pilgrim.

(Nancy⁸, William⁷, William⁶, William⁵, Samuel⁴, John³, William², William¹). William⁵ Bradford, the sixth child of the Hon. Samuel and Sarah (Gray) Bradford, was born at Plympton, in Plymouth County, Mass., Nov. 4, 1729 (O. S.). He studied medicine under the direction of Dr. Ezekiel Hersey, of Hingham, an eminent physician of that time. He married Mary Le Baron, the daughter of Dr. Lazarus Le Baron of Plymouth, Mass., in 1751. He then commenced the practice of medicine in Warren, R. I, and is said to have been highly successful. The town records of Bristol, R. I., show that in 1758 he had become a resident of Bristol. He soon after commenced the study of law. In 1761, he was chosen as a representative for Bristol in the General Assembly.

In 1764 he became Speaker of the House of that body; was Deputy Governor 1775 and 1778, and Senator in Congress from 1793 to 1797. His public record constitutes an important part of the history of Rhode Island.

William⁶ Bradford, of the sixth generation in descent from the Mayflower ancestor, had the title of Major. He was the son of

William Bradford and Mercy (Le Baron) Bradford, and was born in 1752. He married Elizabeth Bloom James in 1777. He died Feb. 29, 1811 ; she died Dec. 30, 1852, aged 74 years.

William[7] Bradford, of the seventh generation, had the title of Captain. He was the son of Major William and Elizabeth Bradford. He was born Feb. 2, 1781. He married Mary Smith, Feb. 1, 1804. He died April 23, 1851. She was born Dec. 10, 1782; died Nov. 6, 1869.

Nancy[8] (Smith) Bradford, daughter of Captain William[7] Bradford and Mary Smith Bradford, his wife, was born April 7, 1811. She married Leonard Wright, April 11, 1830. She died August 31, 1878.

7. Marilla Fiske Gray, b. Feb., 1839, died Nov. 16, 1839.

Robert Gray, the discoverer, was a descendant of Edward Gray of Plymouth. He was born in Tiverton, R. I., in May 1755; died in Charleston, S. C., in 1806. He commanded the Sloop "Washington," which was fitted out with the ship "Columbia," by merchants of Boston for the purpose of trading with the natives on the northwest coast. The vessel sailed on the 30th of September, 1787, and carried with them medals for distribution among the Indians, bearing on one side a ship under sail with the words " Columbia " and Washington commanded by John Kendrick, and on the reverse "fitted out at Boston, North America, for the Pacific Ocean " by encircling six, the proprietors.

He returned in 1790, on the " Columbia," by the way of Canton, China, and was the first man to carry the American flag around the globe. Later he made a second voyage, and on the 11th of May, 1791, discovered the mouth of a great river, to which he gave the name " Columbia," after his own vessel. Subsequently he commanded trading vessels from Boston until his death. Asa Gray, of Tiverton, R. I., from 1820, for several years, held the office of Town Clerk, also was a Justice of the Peace.

For a further notice of the life and illustrious service of Captain Robert Gray, descendant of Edward Gray of Plymouth, the following account is taken from the Boston Journal, under date May 10, 1892. It is entitled " A Memorable Anniversary : "

Today with fitting ceremonies there is being observed in the far-away city of Astoria, Oregon, an anniversary in which Bostonians have an important interest. It is the centenary of the discovery of the great Columbia River by Captain Gray of the ship Columbia of Boston, the first merchantman flying the Stars and Stripes to visit the northwest coast of America, and the first to circumnavigate the world.

The voyage of the Columbia gave a notable evidence of the commercial enterprise and nautical daring of early Boston. The ship and a tender known as the Lady Washington were built in 1787 by Messrs. Barrell, Brown, Bulfinch, Derby, Hatch and Pintard, Boston merchants. The Columbia was 220 tons burden — less than half as large as the average three-masted schooner of the present day — and the Lady Washington was a sloop of 90 tons, about the size of the ordinary Gloucester fisherman's. In these two pigmy vessels a band of bold Boston sailors set out to face the rigors of Cape Horn, the cannon shot of jealous Spaniards (who then claimed sole dominion over the whole Pacific Ocean) and the plots and stratagems of fierce savages.

Captain Kendrick commanded the Columbia and Captain Gray the Lady Washington, when the little squadron set sail from Nantasket Roads, on Oct. 1, 1787. In the South Atlantic they were separated by a storm, and the sloop out-stripped her larger consort and reached Nootka, Vancouver Islands, August 2, 1788, ten months from Boston. The Columbia, which had to put into Juan Fernandez for repairs, did not arrive until nearly two months later. Here Gray and Kendrick, the two captains, exchanged ships and, securing a load of furs by barter with the Indians, the Columbia, under Gray's command, crossed the Pacific to China, and there took a cargo of tea for Boston, reaching her home port in August, 1790. Tradition has it that this first voyage of an American ship around the world was not a profitable one. But our Boston merchants were not daunted by the unfortunate results of their first venture. The Columbia was immediately fitted out again, and sailing from Boston on Sept. 28, 1790, reached the northwest coast for the second time June 5, 1791. Kendrick in the Lady Washington meanwhile had been buying land and trading with the Indians. His deeds he sent by way of China to the State Department at Washington, where they afterward proved of inestimable value in establishing our title to the Northwest.

In the spring of 1792, Gray in the Columbia, and Haswell, his mate, in a small sloop, the Adventure, which had been built during the winter, partly of material brought from Boston — the first American vessel ever launched on the Pacific — set sail on a voyage of discovery. It is an interesting historical circumstance that on April 29, while sailing southward, he met at sea, George Vancouver, the English explorer, who was then coming up the coast; Vancouver had sailed by the Columbia River without seeing it, though the keen-eyed Yankee captain had sighted it as he was sailing northward on

his second voyage from Boston the spring before. Gray generously acquainted
the Englishman with his discovery, and further told him that strong winds
and fierce currents had prevented him from entering the mouth of the great
river. But Vancouver apparently did not realize the significance of the discovery, for the two fleets parted and the American vessels were left to pursue the voyage alone. On May 7, Gray entered an inlet known as Bulfinch
Sound, where he repulsed an attack from the Indians. On May 10 he left
this place, and the following day, aided by favoring breezes, sailed over the
bar into the great river whose entrance he had unsuccessfully attempted a
year before. Anchoring ten miles within the bar, he named the river after
the good ship which had borne him over so many oceans, and, like the true
Bostonian that he was, he also named the jutting points at the harbor's
mouth Cape Hancock and Point Adams. Subsequently he sailed some
twenty miles farther up the river, beyond the site of the present city of
Astoria. ·

This week Astoria is celebrating the achievements of this dauntless
Boston captain and his good crew. Though Gray, who had been in the
Continental Navy, died leaving a widow and children in poverty, and
though Kendrick of the Lady Washington perished with Cook in the
Sandwich Islands and his ship was lost, Boston enterprise followed up the
discoveries of these gallant sailors, and Astoria was founded by Boston merchants in 1810, a year before the first of the Astors began his fur-trading
operations on the northwest coast. A party of the descendants of the brave
Bostonians who first carried the starred flag into these far nothern waters
will join this week in the festivities at Astoria.

The voyage of the Columbia a century ago is memorable not only
because it helped to add a new empire to our mighty national domain, but
because it was the first of those great commercial ventures in distant seas
which years after were to bring tribute to our good city from all quarters of
the globe.

The following beautiful poem in honor of the ancestress, Dorothy
Lettice Gray, wife of Edward Gray, the rich merchant who
settled in Plymouth, Mass. as early as 1643 was written by Mrs.
Mary H. (Gray) Clarke (Nina Gray Clarke), a short time before
her death, which occurred May 30, 1892:

DOROTHY LETTICE.

Dorothy Lettice, sweet Dorothy Lettice,
  Gathering spring flow'rs near old Plymouth rock,
Followed so soon the Mayflower thy footsteps
  They too for first coming persistently knock.

Dorothy Lettice, sweet Dorothy Lettice,
  Raise thy brown eyes, for is passing thy way
The rich merchant whose horse hoofs 'gainst the rocks too are knocking,
  The rich merchant of Plymouth, the Sir Edward Gray.

Why half hide thy face in anemone blossoms,
  Anemone mayflower, sweetest of spring?
Thy smiles are fresh comers with bonnet o'erspreading,
  Thou a mayflower sailing with butterfly wing.

Dorothy Lettice, sweet Dorothy Lettice,
  There's a love tale for thee of ye olden time,
A Lincolnshire plant merrie England has started
  To gain strength in the soil of old Plymouth's rough clime.

Dorothy Lettice, sweet maid of the mayflowers,
  Why watch thy knight 'neath thy brow shading hand?
A fragant breeze whispers, " Though he's old, over thirty,
  I ne'er could say no to a lover so grand."

Toward Dorothy Lettice turns the Sir in his saddle,
  His eager steed bends his proud head to his will;
Quoth the Sir, " I'm thy pilot, my trim little mayflower,
  And through life's roughest waves I will safe guide thee still."

Further researches show that Edward Gray emigrated from England. The Parish Registers of Stapleford Tawney, Essex Co., England, as printed at the Private Press of Frederick Arthur Crisp, Grove Park, Denmark Hill, London, S. E., 1892, furnish the following entries relating to this family,—

Año Dôni 1623. The fifteenth day of Aprill was baptised Edward Graie, soñe of John Graie.

Año Dôni 1621. The twentieth day of Januarie was buried Joshua Graie sône of John Graie.

The twelfth day of ffebruarie was buried Joan Graie daughter of John Graie.

Año Dôni 1608. The eight and twentith daie of August was baptized Richard Graie sonne of John Graie.

Año Dôni 1613. The nineth day of October was buried Richard Graie sone vnto John Graie.

Año Dôni 1616. The first day of Januarie was baptised Sarah Graie, daughter of John Graie.

Año Dôni 1620. The sixteenth day of July was baptised Thomas Graie, sone of John Graie.

Año Dôni 1612. The seauenth day of ffebruarie was baptised John Graie, the sone of John Graie. 1642, the Thirty day of May was Married Thomas Harding and Sarah Gray.

Año Dôni 1610. The fine and twentith day of November was baptized Josua Graye, sone vnto John Graye.

Año Dôni 1615. The foure and twentith day of September was baptised Rebecca Graye, daughter of John *Graie*.

1638. The eight and twentieth day of May was married Thomas Perry and Rebecca Grey.

A John Grey [was] buried the eighth day of March, 1658.

The following is a summary :—

Edward Gray was baptized April 15, 1623; there was in the parish no further record.

Joshua Grey was baptized Nov. 25, 1610, and was buried January 20, 1621.

Joan Gray was buried Feb. 12, 1621; there is in the parish no record of her baptism.

Richard Gray was baptized Aug. 28, 1608, and was buried Oct. 9, 1613.

Sarah Gray was baptized January 12, 1616, and was married to Thomas Harding, May 30, 1642.

Thomas Gray was baptiszed July 16, 1620; he has in the parish no further record.

John Gray another son was baptized Feb. 7, 1612; he has no further record in the parish.

Rebecca Graye was baptized Sept. 24, 1615, and was married to Thomas Perry, May 28, 1638.

A John Gray was buried March 8, 1658. There is no record in the parish of the marriage of John Gray the father of these children, and the name of his wife is not mentioned.

There is no mention or entry of the baptism of his daughter

Joan. It is to be presumed that John Gray was not native of Stapleford Tawney, but was only for some years a resident of that parish.

The record of the christenings of the parish begins in the year 1558; so also do those of the marriages and burials. Stapleford Tawney is a parish in the hundred of Onger in the County of Essex, 3 3-4 miles S. E. by E. from Epping, containing 283 inhabitants. The living is a rectory with that of Mount Theydon, united as an arch-deaconry of Essex and diocese of London, rated in the King's books at £15, 8, 9 and in th epatronage of Sir Thomas Bart. The church is dedicated to Saint Mary. I am unable to give at this writing the name of the father of John Gray living in Stapleford Tawney; he was undoubtedly connected with an important branch of the Gray family that had for many ages been illustrious in the English annals.

The family of Gray or Grey, says Burke in his peerage, claims descent from Rollo (born 860 A. D.) chamberlain to Robert Duke (1027–1035) of Normandy. Rollo had from Robert a grant of the Castle and honor of Croy in Picardy, whence his posterity assumed this surname, which was afterward written Gray or Grey. The orthography of the name is various, Gray having been the usual mode of spelling in ancient times, in England as well as in Scotland.

Rollo was the father of John, Lord of Gray, whose son Anschetil de Gray was one of William the Conqueror's companions in arms at the battle of Hastings, and was recorded in the Doomsday Survey as Lord of many manors and lordships in the counties of Oxford and Buckingham. Anschetil de Gray had two sons, both named John, one of whom was made Archbishop of Canterbury in 1206. He was by King John appointed Lord Deputy of Ireland; he died in 1214. His elder brother, John de Gray, had a son, Henry de Gray, who was high in favor with King Richard I. and King John.

Walter de Gray, who was probably brother of Henry, was made Lord High Chancellor by King John; in the 17th year of that King's reign he was made archbishop of York.

Henry de Gray had several sons.

I. Robert of Rotherfield* whose male line ended in Robert, was Lord Gray of Rotherfield, in the reign of King Richard II.

II. Richard de Gray, whose principal seat was at Cordnor in Derbyshire. He was ancestor of the Lords Grey of Cordnor, whose male line failed in the reign of Henry VII.

III. John, from whom the most illustrious branches of the house of Gray have sprung. He was high in the favor of King Henry III., and died in the fiftieth year of that King's reign. He was father of Reginald, Lord Grey of Wilton and Ruthyn who had issue.

John Lord Grey of Wilton and Ruthyn, who died in the 17th year of King Edward II. He had issue: 1, Henry Lord Grey of Wilton, from whom descended a long line of Lords Grey de Wilton, the last of whom, Thomas Lord Grey de Wilton, died without issue in 1614; his inheritance was carried by Bridget into the family of Egerton, created in 1801 Earl of Wilton. 2, Roger Lord Grey de Ruthyn, the ancestor of the illustrious house of Grey, Earl of Kent. The elder line of this great family failed in Henry Earl of Kent, who died without issue in 1639, when his sister Susan carried the barony Grey de Ruthyn into the family of Longueville, and thence through the Yelvertons, earls of Sussex, into that of the Marquis of Hastings.

The younger line of the earls of Kent attained to ducal rank in the person of Henry, Duke of Kent, in 1710; on his death in 1740, his earldom and dukedom became extinct. He is represented as the co-heir in the female line of Earl de Grey. A younger branch of the Lords Grey de Ruthyn attained to the highest importance. It was founded by Edward Grey, uncle to the first Earl of Kent, who acquired by marriage the barony of Ferrers and of Groby [Leicestershire]. His eldest son, John Lord Grey of Groby, married Elizabeth Wydville, afterward queen of King Edward IV., by whom he had issue, Thomas Grey, created in the 15th year of his age Marquis of Dorset, in 1476, by his step-

---

*Dugdale states that Robert of Rotherfield and Walter, Archbishop of York, were the sons of Henry de Gray, while Collins says that they were his brothers. It would seem from the chronology that Walter at all events must have been brother of Henry (see Burke's note).

father.   His grandson, Henry Marquis of Dorset, married Frances
Brandon, granddaughter to King Henry VII.; he was created
Duke of Suffolk and was beheaded 1554.   His unfortunate
daughter Jane was seated for a few days upon the throne of England.   From his younger brother John the earls of Stamford are
descended.

IV.   William de Grey was seated at Sandiacre, in the County
of Derby, and was ancestor of the Greys of Sutton, whose inheritance passed by a daughter to the family of Leake, Earl of Scarsdale.

V.   Henry de Grey.

These families of Grey bore for arms, barry of six argent and
azure, in chief three torteaux.   There is also a family of that name
of great antiquity in the County of Suffolk, descended from the
same stock and bearing the arms, viz.: De Grey Lord Walsingham, so created in 1780.

Another great branch of the house of Grey has been seated for
ages with baronial rank in the North of England, and have
adopted different armorial bearings, viz.: gules, a lion rampant
with a border engrailed argent.   The ancestor of this family was
Sir John de Grey of Berwycke, in the County of Northumberland;
he was living in 1372.   He was father of Sir Thomas Grey of
Berwycke and Chillingham; he died in 1402, and left issue by Jane,
daughter of John Mowbray, Duke of Norfolk.   There were many
descendants of this stock.

I.   John Grey of Powis.
II.   Thomas Grey of Worke.
III.   The Greys of Scotland.
IV.   Hugo de Grey.
V.   John de Grey.
VI.   Sir Andrew Grey.

It is believed that John Gray of Stapleford Tawney descended
from the Dorset branch of the Gray family.   The Dorset Grays,
as is well known, are of great antiquity, and were for many generations in high favor with the English kings.   Members of this
family were for centuries seated in Westminster and in other
sections in and about London; they attained in older times rank

and position of the highest importance. In the early settlement
of this country members of this family emigrated to New England
and to the British Provinces. Samuel Gray, an early settler of
Boston, was of the Dorset Greys, that trace back their descent, as
has already been stated, to the time of William the Conqueror.

Mary Hannah Gray Clarke, wife of Dr. Augustus P. Clarke,
died Monday afternoon, May 30, 1892, at 4 o'clock, at her residence, 825 Massachusetts Avenue, Cambridge, Mass. Mrs. Clarke
was born March 28, 1835, at Bristol, R. I., and was a daughter of
Gideon and Hannah Orne (Metcalf) Gray. She was a great granddaughter of Col. Thomas Gray of Bristol, R. I., an officer illustrious in the war of the Revolution. She was the seventh in descent
from Edward Gray, who emigrated from Westminster, London,
England, and settled in Plymouth, Mass., as early as 1643.

She attended the public schools of her native town, and became
a pupil in Miss Hannah Easterbrook's school for young ladies.
During her childhood she resided much of the time with her parents on the homestead of her fathers. The family consisted of two
other daughters and of two sons. The two brothers still survive
her. Each of the different members of the family has been connected with an evangelical church, and has lived a well regulated
life and has been strengthened by the blessed assurance of the
Christian's hope.

Her parents were Methodists. Her father united with a church
of that denomination in Bristol, at the age of fourteen years, only
so, however, after confession of faith and immersion. He was
ever regarded by all who knew him as a most devout Christian.

Mrs. Clarke had a maternal aunt, who at an early age married the
Reverend Thomas Wait Tucker, a pioneer Methodist clergyman
of New England. Mrs. Tucker was a woman of an extraordinary
intellectual and Christian turn of mind. She no doubt exercised
a most potent influence over the young girl, not only in the
choice of studies which she was to pursue, but also in imparting
at an early age sound religious teaching, which is often condu-
cive to a healthy spiritual development. For many months at a
time she dwelt as a companion and favorite in the family of her
aunt.

Influenced as she undoubtedly was by the religious instruction of her parents and of her near relatives, at the age of thirteen years, during a season of a revival of religion in Bristol in 1848, she gave evidence of conversion. She pressed on, and at the command of her Lord and Master, following the example of her saintly father, she was baptized at the place in Bristol where the bay opens out toward the blue and broadening ocean and where many a convert had before repaired and been baptized. She then went down into the deep waters and was buried in baptism. She did this, she said, that she might arise into newness of life. The pastor who officiated on that occasion was a dear friend of the family. He had also been educated as a practicing physician.

Mrs. Clarke was naturally of a happy and pleasant disposition. During childhood she was once dangerously ill and for a while was not expected to recover. A few years later she barely escaped drowning when near the Charles River while she was visiting her aunt, Mrs. Tucker, at Watertown, Mass. These incidents in her early life must have deepened her impressions relating to the uncertainty of life, and must have added to her thoughtfulness regarding the necessity of making complete preparation for the life beyond.

Her mother was a woman of uncommon ability. She had long been a school teacher in New London, and in Bristol, R. I. She was of great piety. Perhaps no better compliment can be paid her than by recalling the remark once made concerning her by our own neighbor, Mrs. Eaton, the sister of the late Rev. Lewis Colby. Mrs. Eaton said that she could most profitably sit at the feet of Mrs. Gray, who at that time was past eighty years, and could as a little child learn from her out of her wonderful experience and still more out of her great knowledge of scripture.

Mrs. Clarke had had the rare advantage of an uninterrupted association with her mother during some portion of almost every year until August, 1885, when in the morning, in a moment, in the twinkling of an eye, she passed on, as we trust, to the mansions above.

Mrs. Clarke was the author of many juvenile stories, books, operettas, and lyric poems. She wrote under different pen names, but was known, however, as an author, under the name of Nina Gray Clarke. Some of her works are "Obed Owler and the Prize Writers"; "Effie, Fairy Queen of Dolls"; "Prince Puss-in-Boots"; "Golden Hair and Her Knight of the Beanstalk in the Enchanted Forest."

At the time of her last illness she was engaged in writing in verse the story of Roger Williams. This was an attempt to portray the true spirit of the great Puritan reformer and founder of Rhode Island, as disclosed by his work and more especially by his teaching among the aborigines. It was in the writing of her lyric poems that she manifested to the greatest advantage her indwelling spirit. In writing she ever delighted to make appropriate allusion to the scriptures. In touching pathos she often referred to the circle that gathered in bygone days under her paternal roof. To illustrate more fully her feelings, I quote the following from her poem which she wrote and which was given to the public on Feb. 12, 1872. It was entitled "The Smile of my Father:"

"That smile of my father since borrowed from Heaven,
    Even death has not power to enclose in the tomb,
But to me its pure light forever is given
    To illumine my path in the dark hour of gloom.
Yes! that smile as a beacon shall e'ermore be beaming
    Whate'er sorrows afflict me or dangers surround,
And shall point out the way, whether waking or dreaming,
    To our hereafter home in the bright world beyond."

From another poem, which she wrote and which was published June 2, 1873, some two months after the death of our son Harrison, I extract the following lines:

"Tis of the past the rills now sing,
    And echoes sweet the sad birds bring
Of tones from forms that haunt us now,
    The loved and lost of long ago."

"Sweet June, teach us as years glide by,
    And youth is past and death draws nigh,
To thankful see each lessening year
    The far-off heavens are drawing near."

The following is from another poem written for the Bristol Phœnix, and is called "Angel of Twilight." It opens thus:

"There's a beautiful angel comes gliding at eve,
    And he bathes his bright wings in the Twilight's calm wave,
    And he loosens the thoughts the bright day doth bind,
    Giving rest to the weary and sight to the blind."
                    *   *   *
"O Angel, dear angel, to my own soul come down,
    On whom kindest heaven much mercy hath shown;
    Come lovingly down, bringing ever with thee
    A prayer for the needy, with sweet charity."

The following is from the poem written after the death of her sister Louise:

"How tenderly spring wraps thy tired form to rest,
    While summer spreads o'er thee her blossoming show'rs;
    And may we like thee trust that God knoweth best,
    Having faith we shall meet in life's unfading bow'rs."

The next quotation is from her short poem: "The Bark, the Frailest on the Sea:"

            *   *   *   *   *   *

"My bark is laden deep with love,
    And Faith's the power that can move,
    While Truth alone out-spreads the sail,
    And Hope, the anchor, waits each gale.
    My bark, the frailest on the sea
    Is safe, and bears a bliss for me.
    With treasure such and such to guide,
    The frailest bark stems wind and tide."

After our marriage, Oct. 23, 1861, during my service as surgeon in the war of 1861-1865, Mrs. Clarke tarried part of the time with her parents in Bristol. She also spent much time in Boston. She took a deep interest in the cause of the Union. She employed herself in preparing articles to be sent to the front, and was ever ready to visit and to help those who were sick or wounded in our hospitals. Several of her letters to me while I was in the service are still preserved. They all bear the unmistakable impress of her firm faith in God's providence and in His overruling all things for the best. These letters were ever helpful to me. I am sure without them and the religious fervor they bore I should not have been able to endure so much toil, hardship and privation as I did while in the service.

After the close of the war and our removal to Cambridge, we did not formally unite with any church. Somewhat later we attended for a while the Harvard Methodist church, where was stationed a preacher whom we had long before known in Rhode Island, and who was a warm personal friend of ours. Later still we attended another society. It was not, however, until 1884, on the settling of the Rev. James McWhinnie, D.D., that we turned our faces toward the First Baptist church. We had heard of the Reverend Dr. McWhinnie before he came to Cambridge. We both felt that under his preaching we were making important advance in religious and spiritual understanding. Our new pastor seemed to have all the power and spirit of the old-time masters of the pulpit. Mrs. Clarke was much attached to the church and was always glad to be able to attend the meetings of the sewing circle. She loved the pastor and his family. She was greatly pained on learning the serious nature of his illness, and felt most severely the shock caused by his unexpected death.

Mrs. Clarke always thoroughly enjoyed the privileges of divine service in the house of worship. When abroad she felt it to be a great source of enjoyment to attend on the Sabbath some kind of religious meeting. Whoever in her presence spoke ill of the Bible and of its noble teachings did so only at the loss of her respect. She was not afraid of the infidel. Her wit and sarcasm always proved an insurmountable barrier against such impious attacks.

Mrs. Clarke was a lover of music. She had the gift of song to an unusual degree. She composed several pieces of music as well as the words adapted to their use.

In her remarks made during her serious illness, which extended back for more than a year, she often referred to the " beautiful city," and of the final meeting together of the friends of the redeemed, and expressed that being buried in baptism and rising out of the water were a fit emblem not only of the purifying of the soul, but also of the bursting asunder of the gates and bars of death.'

She was a true and confiding wife, a true mother, a true friend to the needy, with love for all, and with malice toward none. She has gone from us. She has left a priceless legacy, a stainless record, and an all-inspiring example for good work, for noble purpose and for genuine Christian fellowship. She had faith above measure in the righteous promises of God, faith in Christ as revealed by His word, and as exemplified in the lives of that countless army of the redeemed who have lived as witnesses to His truth.

As she realized more and more that this world was fast receding from her view, the hidden mysteries of truth seemed more open to her vision. The reading of the scriptures to her was more comforting; the voice of praise and of song was indeed solacing. She finally fell asleep, bearing in her latest thoughts, as she had before whispered in my ear, the deep conviction and firm faith that she should live again, that she should be raised to the joyous greetings and to a never ending day.

The above, relating to Mrs. Clarke, was written for the records of the First Baptist Church of Cambridge, by her husband, Dr. Augustus P. Clarke, of Cambridge, Mass., June 24, 1892.

CORNU MEAE SALUTIS DE SUPER VENIT.

ARMS OF HORNE.

The arms here presented are from the ancient genealogical records of England. The quartering is with Hendley, whose heiresses were married into the Horne family. The following is the description :—

Arms.—Quarterly, 1st and 4th, gules, a fesse vair, for Horne.

2d and 3d.—Paly, bendy, gules and azure, eight martlets, in orle, or, for Hendley.

Crest of Horne.—An owl proper.

Crest of Hendley.—A martlet or.

The motto, " Cornu mei salutis de super venit,"—" The horn of my salvation cometh from above," was not originally given, but has since been added.

Branches of this family were seated in Kent, Norfolk, Sussex, Middlesex, Leicester, and in other counties of England.

HORNE GENEALOGY.

Though the name Horne is of considerable antiquity in the British annals, the name Orne does not appear. In manuscript No. 60 of the old genealogical pedigrees of Kentish families, also in those of York, numbers 213-224, appears the name of Horne. Richard Horne is found in the old writs of Parliament as "Placide de quo warranto." (See Bardsley's English Surnames, London.)

In that part of France, formerly called Normandy, Orne is the name of a river that flows into the English Channel. In old French, the name of the river was "Olernæ" and also "Olina." In the more modern French, the name was contracted into Orne,* which has been affixed to a department of Normandy in the northwest of France.

In New England the earliest known record which we have of Orne is that of John Horne, who settled in Salem in 1630. According to Savage, John Horne came in the fleet with Winthrop, though he may have been here at an earlier date; he became a freeman in Salem, 18 May, 1631; he was a deacon and Bentley says that in 1680, he required an assistant, since he had been in that office above fifty years. In the earliest records of Salem his name is spelled "Horne." He died in 1680, and left a will,

---

* "Of the names and Arms of the forty soldiers of King William the Conqueror with as many monks," (Plate III, vol. 1, p. 252) is "Eucas de Novo Burgo, with Olane, the holy Monk of the Monastery." (See Fuller's Church History). Olane, the name of one of the great soldiers of the king's retinue, is the nearest in form of any to that of Orne. Inasmuch as holy monks in that early age were not addicted to marriage † and the name in the illustrious families was not continued, it is to be presumed that it had no connection with families by the name of Horne or Orne.

† I am not unaware that Chaucer says that monks did sometimes marry; he does not say this of holy monks, or of such as were of the king's household. Hollinshed mentions as among those who came with William the Conqueror an "Orinal," and Stow in his Chronicle has "Orinall." These names and many others that have been given in the lists are believed to have been fabricated by the old monks, and not to have been names of real persons who came over to England at the time of the Conquest.

which he had signed as "John Orne." Since that date his descendants have signed their name as Orne, as appears from the records preserved by the town clerks of Salem and of other places.

The following is gleaned from the parish register of St. James, Clerkenwell, London, England :

Dec. 27, 1565, Thomas Horner, son of John Horner, was christened.

Richard Horne, son of Thomas Horne, was christened Nov. 19, 1598.

John Horne, son of John Horne, was christened Sept. 11, 1608.

William Horne, son of John Horne, was christened in St. James Clerkenwell, London, June 9, 1609.

Bartholomew and Clement, sons of William Horne, a bastard, was christened Feb. 26, 1632.

Danyel Horne, son of Mr. Edward Horne (Horner), gent., and Frances his wife, was christened Jan. 1, 1621, in St. James Clerkenwell, London.

Allen Horne, son of John Horne, was buried at St. James, Clerkenwell, Sept. 5, 1601.

April 7, 1661, at St. James, Clerkenwell, was christened George Horne, son of Henry Horne.

Oct. 24, 1675, at St. James, Clerkenwell, was christened Mary, daughter of Richard Horne.

Oct. 4, 1596, in the same parish, was christened Joane, daughter of Jerome Horne.

Dec. 20, 1685, at the same parish, was christened Thomas Horne, son of Thomas Horne and Judith Arnold, his wife.

The record at Clerkenwell that John Horne was christened September 11, 1608, and that William Horne was christened June 9, 1609, is in accordance with a family tradition that the ancestors John Horne, of Salem, and William Horne, who early settled at Dover, N. H., had both emigrated from London, England.

There is no evidence thus far to show that either of these persons emigrated from Scotland or was of French descent, as some of the descendants have thought the name indicated.

It is well known that in some parts of England the letter "H" in certain words and names, as hospital and humble, is not sounded, while in other words not commencing with " H " a strong aspirate sound like that in " H " is frequently employed. Our ancestors were not always as particular in writing their names as have been some of their descendants. In regard to the origin of the name of Orne in N. H., it may be remarked that Isaiah Horne and his family, by act of Legislature, in 1807, changed their name to Orne. They then settled in Wolfboro; since that date the descendants have borne the name of Orne.

William Horne, the first one of the family in Cocheco, the Indian name for Dover, N. H., was taxed 0. 4s. 0 in 1659. He lived on Horne's Hill on 6th street; he bought 240 acres of land of Elder Edward Starbuck, September 20, 1661. He was killed in the Indian massacre at Dover, June 28, 1689; inventory entered by his widow 15 July, 1699; his wife's name was Elizabeth. She was taken captive by the Indians, September 80, 1707. Savage says that Elizabeth, the wife of William Horne was from Salisbury, and that she may have married John Waldron after the death of her husband, William Horne, of Dover.

The children of William Horne and Elizabeth, his wife, were:
1. Elizabeth[2], b. 1, 12 mo., 1661, in Salisbury, Mass. (as by Salisbury records).
2. John[2], b. Oct. 25, 1663 (as by N. H. records).
3. Joseph[2], b. (probably about 1666), was dead in 1717.
4. Mary[2], b. ——, * (1673).
5. William[2], b. May 11, 1674; d. without any children, April 12, 1697; he was of Dover.
6. Thomas[2], b. Nov. 28, 1676.
7. Margaret[2], b. May 10, 1679; died, April 12, 1697.
8. Mercy[2], b. (1681), m. Joseph Evans, April 6, 1704.

Of the children of Joseph Horne (of the second generation) was a son William[3] Horne, who had wife Margaret.

Of the children of William[3] Horne and his wife Margaret were:
Joseph[4] Horne, b. (probably about 1724).
Elenor[4] Horne, b. 17 July, 1726.

---

* Tradition says that Mary Horne at the age of only 13 years was married to John Hays, 28 June, 1686.

William⁴ Horne, b. 30 Dec., 1788.

James⁴ Horne, b. 18 January, 1730-31.

From the records of the town clerk of York, Maine, we find the following :

"Joseph Horne (Joseph Horne⁴), his children born in York, of his wife Temperance, the daughter of Thomas Adams,* viz. :

Hannah Horne, born June 3, 1755.

Thomas Horne, born Nov. 26, 1756.

Sarah Horne, born Sept. 19, 1758.

Temperance Horne, born Dec. 19, 1761.

William Horne, born April 10, 1767.

Sarah Horne, born Aug. 16, 1772.

His son Joseph⁵ Horne was born 1751, in Wells, before their removal from Wells to York.

Joseph⁵ Horne married Sarah Jillson† by whom he had three sons and one daughter. Samuel, the eldest, died at sea. David, a lad, stepped on a piece of glass which brought on lockjaw, of which he died suddenly. Lydia, the daughter, a little girl, fell down and cut a vein or artery and bled to death. Joseph⁶ was the youngest; he learned a trade (the blacksmith's) and was a farmer. After the death of his wife Sarah, he is said to have married Elizabeth Jennings and by her to have had a son John who went to Montreal, also a son Andrew and a daughter Elizabeth, and perhaps other children.

Joseph⁵ Horne was, according to Bourne's History of Wells and Kennebunk, Maine, page 483, a member of Captain Samuel Sayer's Maine Company that served in the War of the Revolution (1775–1781). Joseph⁵ Horne‡ was a brave and tried soldier; in 1775 he was with General Benedict Arnold in his dreadful winter march through the Maine wilderness to Quebec.

The following is taken from the Archives in the State Department in Boston, Mass. :

Joseph Horn, private, Lexington alarm Noah M. Littlefield's

---

*A descendant of Henry Adams, of Braintree, Mass., ancestor of the two Presidents of the United States of that name.

†A descendant of Nathaniel Jillson of S. Attleborough, Mass., born there January 24, 1675; died at Smithfield, R. I., May 9, 1751 (married 1700, Elizabeth).

‡See Itinerant Preaching, page 11, by Thomas W. Tucker, 1872.

Co., Col. Moulton's regiment, which marched on the alarm April 19, 1775 from Wells. Length of service 5 days.

Muster roll—Captain Sayer's Co., Col. Scammon's Regiment, dated August 1, 1775. Time of enlistment, May 3, 1775. Time of service, 3 months 4 days. Town to which soldier belonged, Wells, Maine, 3 months' service, vol. 16, p. 27.

Joseph[5] Horn appears in a descriptive list of enlisted men, belonged to Wells, age 30 years (born 1751 in Wells), stature 5 feet, 6 inches, complexion dark, hair dark, eyes ——, occupation husbandman, time of enlistment April 10, 1778, term 3 years. Captain John Pray's Co., Col. Joseph Vose's 1st regiment. (Remarks on the descriptive list) birthplace Wells. Dated West Point, January 1st, 1781, enlisted by Lieutenant Samuel Wells, at Wells, Maine. Muster and Pay-roll.

Joseph Horn appears with rank of private on the Continental Army pay accounts of Captain — Co., Col. Sprout's regiment, for service from April 10, 1778, to December 31, 1777,—credited to Town Wells. Reported in the Major's Company. No Captain given. Continental Army, Books vol. 12, part 2, page 22. Joseph Horn appears with rank of private on the Continental Army pay account of Captain J. Pray's Co., Col. Sprout's regiment for service from January, 1780 to December 31, 1780. Credited to the Town of——, residence in Wells.

Continental Army books, vol. 12, part 1, page 41.

Joseph Horn appears with rank of private on Muster roll of Captain John Pray's Co., Col. Joseph Vose's 1st regiment, 1781, for January 1781—enlisted April 10, 1778, for 3 years. Roll dated at West Point vol. 50, page 7—Worcester Rolls.

Joseph Horn, private, Muster roll of John Pray's Co., Col. Joseph Vose's 1st regiment, Feb. and March, 1781, enlisted April 10, 1778, for 3 years.

Joseph Horn, private, Captain Sayer's Co., Col. Scammon's regiment, Wells, Maine, date not given; probably August return. Reported,—enlisted May, 3, 1775. Coat rolls eight months' service.

Vol. 56, page 205.

Joseph Horn, private, on pay abstract of Lt. Col. Sprout's 12th regiment, for three months' service in the year 1780, in the Massachusetts line of the Continental Army. Books: abstract of rolls, Vol. 31, page 10. Joseph Horn in Col. Ebenezer Sprout's regiment,—time for 3 years. Books Militia returns, Vol. 28, p. 186.

Joseph Horn appears in a list of men mustered in York County, service in Captain Daniel Merrill's Co., Col. Samuel Brewer's regiment, by a return, Wells, April 27, 1778, by Nath[1]. Wells' Muster roll—Place of residence *Sanford*,—term of enlistment 3 years; Record,—state and Continental Counties. May Muster and pay rolls, Vol. 43, p. 125.

Joseph Horn appears, with the rank of private, Muster and pay roll of Captain James Littlefield's Co., Col. Storer's regiment.

Time of enlistment, August 14, 1777.

Time of discharge, Nov. 30, 1777.

Time of service, 4 months and 3 days.

Served in the Northern Army.

Discharged at Queame's Heights, 15 days' travel included.

The name of Joseph Horn appears among signatures* to an order for Bounty Coat, or the equivalent in money, for the eight months' service in 1775 in Captain Samuel Sayer's Co., Col. James Scammon's 30th regiment, dated Cambridge, Oct. 27, 1775.

Payable to Captain Sayer, Coat Rolls, eight months' service· Vol. 57, p. title 21.

Joseph[6] Orne (Horn), (Joseph[6], Joseph[5], Joseph[4], William[3], Joseph[2], William[1]), married November, 1793, Jane Metcalf, a descendant of Michael Metcalf of Norwich, England, and of Dedham, Mass. She was born in Leicester, Mass., July 30, 1776.

The children of Joseph[6], Orne (Horne) and † Jane[6] (or Jennie)

---

* A facsimile of Joseph Horn's signature *[signature]* [reduced one-half]

as made in 1775, is here reproduced from a muster and pay roll found in the Mass. Military Archives.

† Jane(6) Metcalf was married to Joseph Orne, Nov., 1793. Jane(6) Orne was the daughter of Samuel(6) Metcalf, and Hannah his wife. Hannah, the mother of Jane(6), was the daughter of Thomas and Jane Richardson of Leicester, Mass. Mrs. Jane Richardson was the daughter of Captain Nathaniel Downing and his wife Margaret Pynchon; both of whom were of illustrious descent.

William Pynchon, the ancestor of Jane Pynchon, is mentioned by the Indian Apostle, the Rev. John Eliot, in his record of the church of Roxbury, Mass. John Eliot says that " William Pynchon came in the first company ; 1630 he was one of the first foundation of the church at Rocksborough. Mr. William Pynchon was chosen

(Samuel[6], Ebenezer[5], Eleazar[4], Michael[3], Michill[2]) Metcalf were Mary (called also Polly or Dolly) Orne, born in Corinth, Vt., Oct. 15, 1794; she married Rev. Thomas Wait Tucker.

Ebenezer[7] Orne, born Corinth, Vt., April 11, 1796.

Hannah[7] Orne, born in Corinth, Vt., Nov. 19, 1798; she married Gideon Gray, and died in Bristol, R. I., Aug. 14, 1885.

Samuel[7] Orne, born in Corinth, Vt., May 7, 1800.

Solomon[7] Orne, born in Corinth, Vt., Oct 2, 1801.

Joseph[7] Orne, 3d, born June 23, 1805.

Epithis[7] Smith Orne, born Oct. 8, 1808.

Robert[7] S. Orne, born Oct. 10, 1810; died Dec. 1, 1895, and was buried in Bristol, R. I.

Ralph[7] Metcalf Orne, born Jan. 25, 1813.

Roslinda[7] Orne, born April 19, 1815.

Emeline[7] Cushing Orne, born Feb. 29, 1820, married Otis King.

George[7] W. Orne, born Dec. 1, 1823.

Joseph[7] Orne, was married in Corinth, Vt., Nov. 13, 1826, to Elizabeth Anne Cox. (Town record, says Carr.)

Joseph[6] Orne died in Albany, Vt., in 1845.

Mrs. Jane (Jennie) died in Bristol, R. I., March, 1860.

The following entries relating to the Horne family are from the early Dover, N. H., Town records:

"Sarah Horne, daughter of Thomas Horne* by his wife

---

an Assistant yearly, so long as he lived among us ; his wife dyed soone after he landed at New England ; he brought four children to N. E. Ann, Mary, John, Margret. After some years, he married mris Frances Samford, a grave matron of the church at Dorchester. When so many removed from these parts to Plant Conecicot rivr, he also wth othr company went thithr, and planted at a place called Agawam, and was recommended to the church at windsor, on Conecticott, untill such time as it should please God to pvide yt they might enter into church estate among themselves. His daughter Ann was married to mr Smith, sone to mrs Samford by a former husband, he was a Godly, wise young man, and removed to Agawam with his parents. His daughter mary was married to mr Hollioke, the son of mr Hollioke of Linn: mr Pinchons ancient friend.

" Afterwards he wrote a Dialogue concerning Justification, wcb was printed anno 1650, stiled the meritorious price, a book full of error and weakens, and some heresies wch the Generall Court of ye Massachusetts Condemmed to be burnt, and appointed mr John Norton, then Teacher at Ipswich, to confute ye errors contained therein."

" mrs Frances Pinchon, the wife of mr willia Pinchon ; she was a widdow, a matron of the church at Dorchester. wr mr Pinchon married her, she came with the first company, ano, 1630." [See Record Com. 6th Report Roxbury Records.]

* Thomas was son of William [1], the first in Dover.

Judeth * was born in douer (Dover), the 14th day of January, 1699."

"William Horn, sonn of Thomas Horn, by his wife Judeth, was born in douer (Dover) the 7th day of november, 1702."

"Thomas Horn, sonn of Thomas Horn, by his wife Judeth, was born in douer (Dover) the 23d day of october, 1705."

"Ichabod Horn, sonn of Thomas Horn, by his wife Judeth, was born in douer (Dover) the 25th of June, 1710."

"Mary Horne, Dafter of Dannill Horne, by his wife Mary, borne the 13 of April, 1724."

"Elener Horne, Dafter of William Horne, by his wife Margaret, borne the 17th of July, 1726."

"Benjamin Horne, son of Daniel Horne, by his wife Mary, borne the 14 Day of January, 1726."

---

* The following is taken from the Maine Genealogist and Biographer of Augusta, Maine, June, 1877.

Two brothers, George and Maturin Ricker came from England to Dover, N. H. George appeared there in 1670, and was first taxed in 1672, at Cochecho [Cocheco]. Tradition in the family says that he came over with old Parson Reyner and at his expense; and that after repaying the Parson, his next earnings went to get his younger brother Maturin over; Maturin was not taxed in 1672, and the next lists are lost. But as to the Reyner matter the difficulty is that the Parson came over in 1635 and died early in 1669. However, he owned landed property in England, and perhaps this tradition may give a clue to the Rickers as to the place they came from. George settled in what is now Rollingsford, near the Wentworth property. In fact he and John Wentworth (the Elder's son) traded in land somewhat. Maturin must have lived near both of them. George and Maturin were killed by the Indians, June 4, 1706. The original journal of John Pike, who was minister at Dover, which is in the Library of the Massachusetts Historical Society, says under date of June 4, 1706, George Riccer and Maturin Riccor, of Cocheco, were slain by the Indians. George was killed while running up the lane near the garrison ; Maturin was killed in his field, and his little son [Noah] was carried away. The "garrison" was Heard's which stood in the garden of the late Friend Bangs. The "lane" was the present cross-roads just at the southern base of Garrison Hill. George Ricker married Elenor Evans. Her father had been killed by the Indians, doubtless the Mr. Evans whom Pike mentions as killed in the massacre, in the times of profound peace. Rebecca Ricker is now living in Lebanon, Maine, whose grandfather was ten years old when his father, the emigrant was killed, and much older when his mother, Elenor Evans, died. Rebecca says that the Indians chained Mr. Evans to Mr. Waldron's barn as they set it on fire and he was burned to death. He also says that Elenor's brother was killed at that time, and records sustain her assertion ; but this may not be quite correct, inasmuch as a young John Evans appears by other documents to have been taken prisoner, then who died a captive not long after. He was doubtless among the killed. George Ricker by his wife Elenor had nine children, as follows: Judith, b. Feb. 1. 1681. She was once captive. Pike says 26 July, 1696 ; "Being sacrament day. In ambush of Indians laid between Capt. Gerrish's field and Tobias Hansom's orchard, shot upon the people returning from meeting; killed, Nicholas Otis, Mary Downs, and Mary Jones; wounded, Richard Otis, Anthony Lauden and Experience Heard ; took John Tucker, Nicholas Otis's wife and Judith Riccar." Belnap adds that the captives were taken to Penobscot, but they soon found their way home. This ambush was almost precisely where the Congregational church stands. Judith was home again 14 April, 1699, for on that day Parson Pike married her to Thomas Horne. She had four children,—Sarah, Ichabod, Thomas and William, and was ancestress of various Horne families still flourishing. But she died, and he married Esther ——, and had five more children.

" Judeth Horne, Dafter of Thomas Horne, sen^r by his wife Ester, borne the 16th of august, in the year 1721."

" Margrett Horn, by his wife Ester, born the 16th of aprill, 1722."

" Samuell Horn, by his wife Ester, borne the 16th of february, 1724."

" Abigal Horne, by his wife Ester, borne the 7th Day of December, 1725."

" Dreusila Horne, Dafter of Thomas Horne, by his wife Ester, borne ye 18th of June, 1727,"

" Paul Horne, the son of Danil Horn, by his wife Mary, Born 24th May, 1730."

" Abigail Horn, the Daughter of Daniel Horne, by his wife Mary, Born March ye 28th, 1734."

" William Horn, ye son of Wm. Horn, By his wife Margaret, Born the 30 Dec., (?) 1728."

" James Horn ye son of Wm. Horn, by his wife Margret, Born 18 Jan^ry, 1730-31."

" Esther Horn, Daughter of Thomas Horn, by his wife Esther, Born April 26th, 1729."

" Paul Horn, son of Thomas Horn, By his wife Esther, Born septem^r 5th, 1737."

" William Horne and Jane Davis, Were Joyned together in marriage by Joseph Hanson Esq. (?) the 14th day of July, 1756."

" Elizabeth Horn, Daughter of Nathaniel Horn by his wife Sarah, was born in Dover February ye 15th, 1738-9."

" Sarah Horn, the daughter of Nathaniel Horn by his wife Sarah, born in Dover, August 13th, 1742."

"Hannah Horn, Daughter of Nathaniel Horn by his wife Sarah, Born in Dover, Septem^er 24th, 1745."

MARRIAGES.

1777, Feb 11, Caleb Horn and Molly Randel, both of Somersworth.

1777, April 8, James Chesley and Lydia Horn.

1778, March 8, Michael Reade and Deborah Horn.

1781, Jany 31, Samuel Heard Horn and Hannah Vicker.

1782, July 10, Jonathan Horn and Elizabeth Peaslee.

1784, March 14, David Twomby and Mary Horn.

William Horne died in Dover, 1815, said to be aged 95 (though probably only 87).

William Horne, a friend, married 9.10 mo. (October) 1713, Mary Varney, and had Sarah ; b. 1, 6 mo. 1714, who married 31, 5 mo., 1734, Isaac Hanson.

Daniel Horne had also by wife Mary,——Daniel, b. 23d Oct., 1716, Ichabod b. 5th March, 1720-21.

A Daniel Horne died 7 April, 1777, aged 88 years.

The names of the children of John Orne (Horne), of Salem, according to Savage, were as follows :

Recompense, baptized 25 Dec., 1636; Jonathan, 1 August, 1658; both died before their father; besides these were the following, who outlived him: John, Simon, b. 28 October, 1649, Joseph, Benjamin, Eliz. Gardner, Johanna Harvey, Mary Smith, and Ann Felton, b. 22 March, 1657. We may presume, says Savage, that his wife was Ann, since that name appears in Felt's list of the earliest names of the Church.

Ann Eliz. Horne died at Newbury, says Coffin, 6 May, 1672. All descendants in our day, continues Savage, spell their name as Orne (as did he in his last will). Nine by the name of Orne are counted among the graduates of Harvard. Joseph is the son from whom is our best known stock. Chandler speaks in his Family Genealogy of Lois Orne and gives the following record :

William Paine, b. 5 June, 1750, d. 19 April, 1833, in Worcester, m. at Salem, Mass., 22 Sept., 1773. Lincoln's papers say m. at Hampton Falls, 23 Sept., 1773, by license from His Excellency, J. Wentworth.

Miss Lois[5] Orne, d. of Timothy[4] Orne of Salem, by his wife Rebecca Taylor of Lynn. Timothy[4] Orne was son of Timothy[3] Orne, who married Lois Pickering, daughter of John[3] and Sarah (Burrill) Pickering, and he was son of John[2] and Alice (Flint) Pickering, and he was son of John and Elizabeth Pickering. He, Timothy[3] was son of Joseph[2] Orne, who m. Ann Thompson, and he was son of John and Ann Horne. She, Lois Orne, was a young lady with a fortune of £3000. The services of plate (magnificent for our own as well as for ancient days) which Miss Orne brought into the Paine family attest the solidity of her fortune and the lustre of her descent, bearing the oft repeated broad shield and the ducal coronet of the princely house of Horne. Her miniature was at the house of Joseph S. Talbot, Esq., Salem, Mass. She died 27 Feb., 1822, at Worcester, Mass., aged 66.

It is to be regretted that the author of this singular record did not make further mention concerning this "princely house of Horne," whether it were located in London or Salem.

Reference to Webber's and Nevin's History of Salem, page 59, will show that John Orne, the "illustrious ancestor of this princely house," was merely a house carpenter, for it is there stated he was employed to build a house which was to be occupied by Hugh Peters. This was about 1651. The following entries in relation to John Orne (Horne) of Salem, Mass., have been received from the city clerk of that ancient municipality, and includes all the entries of this family prior to 1750 :—

Jonathan son of Jo^n Horne bo., 28 : 5 : 58., and dyed 11 : 7 : 58.

John Horne and Mary Clarke were maried by Major Denison, 30 of October, 1667. Daughter Mary borne the 23 of August 1668 and died the 20 : 6mo 1669.

John Horne, his daughter Sara born by Mary his wife ye 26 : 12mo, 1669.

Theire daughter Elizabeth borne ye 27 : 10mo 1671.

Dau. Abigaile borne 20 : 6mo 1673—Son John borne the 6th of 9mo 1675.

Daughter Mary borne ye 25 : 7mo 1678 :

Their son Samuell borne the 29, May 1682.—His son Ebenezer bo., 29 : 6 : 84.

Symond Horne and Rebecka Stevens widdow were married the 28 of February 1675. Theire son Josiah borne the middle September, 1677. Son Symond borne ye 11 : 11mo : 1679.

Jonathan Horne son of John Horne and Naomi his wife deceased Octob^r 6, 1701.

Joseph Horne, Anna Tomson were married ye 12 : 5mo : 1677.

Theire daughter Anna borne the 14 Aprill, 1678.—

Mercy ye daughter of Benj^a Horne borne 24th Jan^r 1684.

His daught^r. Margarett borne y^e 22nd Novemb^r. 1687.

Mary y^e wife of John Horne departed this life y^e 19th day of June, 1690.

Lynn Records.

Benj^a. Horne deceas^d. Sept. 13th 1702.

Mercy Horne daught^r of Benj. and Sarah Horne born Jan. 4, 168$\frac{4}{5}$.

Their daughter Margaret born Nov. 22, 1687.

Their son Benj^a. born March 14, 169$\frac{4}{5}$.

Jon^a Orne son of Jn Orne and Naomy his wife, was borne 22 November 1693.

Recompence Orne son of John Orne and Naomy his wife borne at Salem January the 20th 169$\frac{5}{6}$.

David Orne son of John Orne and Naomy his wife borne Salem 13 March 1698.

Samuel Orne son of Timothy and Lois Orne born Novr 1710.

Salem Records.

Clark Gaton Pickman married Sarah, daughter of Mr. Timothy Orne, and died in 1781, aged 36 years (date of marriage not given.)

Lewis Hunt married 1st Sarah Orne and 2nd Mary Bowditch (date of mar. not given).

John Cabot and Hannah Orne, were married October 29th 1702.

Their daughter Susanna, born July the 1st between 8 and 9 of the o'clock in the morning, anno 1703.

Their son John born October 26th between 9 and 10 of the o'clock at night anno 1704.

Their daughter Esther born the 11th of June 1706.

Their daughter Mary born June 4th 1709.

Their daughter Anna born the 8th of March 17$\frac{10}{11}$.

Their daughter Margaret born June 14th 1713.

Their daughter Elizabeth born June 12th 1715.

Their son Francis born May 22^d 1717.

Mr. Timothy Orne married to Miss Lois Pickering April the 7th 1709.

Their son Samuel born November 7th 1710 and deceased March 7th 17$\frac{10}{11}$.

Their daughter Lois born March 16th 17$\frac{11}{12}$.

Their daughter Esther born January 18th 17$\frac{14}{15}$.

Their son Timothy born June 27th 1717.

Their son Samuel born January 8th 17$\frac{19}{20}$.

Their daughter Mary born February 28th 17$\frac{21}{2}$.

Their daughter Eunice born January 9th 1725.

Their daughter Eunice deceased February 8th 1725.

Their son John born June 16th 1731.

Joseph Grafton and Mary Orne married Feb'y 13th 17$\frac{18}{19}$.

Their son Joseph born August 14th 1721.

Their son Joseph deceased October 4th 1721.

Their daughter Susannah born July 29th 1722.

Their daughter Mary born January 15th 17$\frac{24}{5}$.

Their son Joseph born August 26th 1726.

Their daughter Anne born December 24th 1727.

Their daughter Esther born June 6th 1729.

October 22^d 1677, John Smith of Charlestown and Maria Horne of Salem, married by Moses Maverick, Commissioner at Marblehead.—*Charlestown Record.*

Mr. John Cabbot and Mrs. Anna Orne married October 29th 1702, by Mr. Nichols Noyes.

Daniel Lambert and Margaret Horne married May 6th 1708, by Mr. Nichols Noyes.

Benjamin Eaton and Marcey Orne married November 24th 1709, by Mr. Nichols Noyes.

Joseph Grafton and Mary Orne married February 13th 17$\frac{18}{19}$, by the Rev^d. W. Samuel Fisk.

Benjⁿ Orne and Eliza King married November 5th 1721 by the Rev^d. Benjamin Prescott.

Mr. Thomas Lee and Mrs. Lois Orne, both of Salem married December 29th 1737 by the Rev^d. Samuel Fisk.

Mr. Samuel Gardner and Mrs. Esther Orne both of Salem married December 13th 1738 by the Revd. Samuel Fisk.

Josiah Orne and Sarah Elvins, both of Salem married July 18th 1744, by Revd. James Dimon.

Mr. Jonathan Orne and Miss Elizabeth Putnam both of Salem married June 28, 1748, by Revd. John Sparhawk.

The following in relation to the Orne (Horne) family has also been received from the town clerk of Marblehead :—

Nov. 23d 1704, Joshua Orne to Elizabeth Norman, by Rev. Sam'l Cheever.

July 18th 1728, Joshua Orne, Jr., to Sarah Gale, by Rev. John Barnard.

Oct. 26th 1730, John Brown to Elizabeth Orne, by Rev. John Barnard.

Mar. 15, 1743, Joshua Orne, Jr., to Agnes Gallison, by Rev. John Barnard.

July 10, 1744, John Orne to Abigail Conant, by Rev. John Barnard.

Nov. 8, 1757, Samuel Orne to Sarah Preble, by Rev. John Barnard.

Dec. 1, 1757, Thos. Richardson to Elizabeth Orne, by Rev. John Barnard.

April 29, 1760, William Homan to Rebecca Orne, by Rev. John Barnard.

Jan. 27, 1754, Azor Orne to Mary Coleman, by Rev. John Barnard.

Dec. 19th, 1765, Lewisden Bowden to Sarah Orne, by Rev. Wm. Whitwell.

Sept. 18, 1766, Richard Richardson to Sarah Orne, Rev. Wm. Whitwell.

Sept. 16th, 1730, Simon Orne to Mary Osgood, Rev. John Barnard.

Oct. 20th, 1768, Jonathan Orne to Priscilla Holgate, Rev. John Emerson.

Jan. 25, 1775, Nathaniel Raymond to Elizabeth Orne, Rev. W^m. Whitwell.

Sept. 29, 1777, Joshua Orne, Esqr., to Mary Lee, Rev. W^m. Whitwell.

Oct. 4, 1777, Jonathan Orne to Mary Collins, Rev. W^m. Whitwell.

Dec. 23, 1771, Joshua Orne Esq. to Mary Stacey, Rev. W^m. Whitwell.

March 8, 1774, James Trefry to Rebekah Orne, Rev. W^m. Whitwell.

April 23, 1786, Hon. Azor Orne to Mrs. Mary Orne, by Samuel Sewall, Esq.

Nov. 10th, 1782, John Reed Malcolm to Mrs. Rebekah Orne.

Aug. 14, 1783, Capt. Joshua Orne to Lucretia Bourn, Rev. Ebenezer Hubbard.

Dec. 29th, 1785, Azor Orne to Sally Gerry, Rev. Ebenezer Hubbard.

Nov. 1st, 1789, Joshua Prentiss, Jr., to Elizabeth Russell Orne, Rev. Isaac Story.

Sept. 3rd, 1793, John Orne to Mary Pearce, by Rev. Ebenezer Hubbard.

July 12, 1795, Jonathan Orne Jr. to Anna Harris, Rev. Ebenezer Hubbard.

Sept. 24, 1797, John Orne to Sally Green, Rev. Ebenezer Hubbard.

Aug. 8th, 1798, Aaron O. Kitchens to Mary Orne, Rev. Ebenezer Hubbard.

BIRTHS.

March 30th, 1710. Son to Joshua and Elizabeth.

Oct. 22, 1722. John, son of Joshua and Elizabeth.

Sept. 22, 1723. John, son of Joshua and Elizabeth.

Aug. 6, 1726, Benjamin, son of Joshua and Elizabeth.

Jan. 23, 1728. Caleb, son of Joshua and Elizabeth.

April 6, 1755. Sarah, dau. of Azor and Mary.

Nov. 18, 1757. Joshua, son of Azor and Mary.

March 2nd, 1761. Azor, son of Azor and Mary.

DEATHS.

Dec. 14, 1722. John, son of Joshua and Elizabeth,1-1-23.
Aug. 23, 1725. Benjamin, son of Joshua and Elizabeth, 17.
Sept. 1st, 1728. Caleb, son of Joshua and Elizabeth, 7-8,
Jan. 12, 1810. Abagail Orne. Single.
Dec. 2nd, 1818. Lucretia, widow of Col. Joshua Orne.
April 19th, 1820. Azor Orne, son of Col. Joshua Orne, killed in a duel.
Sept. 23, 1820. Jonathan, son of John, 14 years.
March, 1821. Oliver, son of Joshua and Lucretia.
Mar. 25, 1825. Abagail P., wife of John Orne, Jr.
Dec. 16, 1826. Nancy, widow of Jonathan, 60 years.
March 31st, 1827. John Orne, 61 years.
Sept. 25, 1833. Jonathan Orne, age 37 years.
June 30, 1835. Mary, wife of John Orne, 80 years, 6 months.
March 11, 1843, Ann Orne, 25 years.
Aug. 8, 1846. Sarah Orne, 76 years.
Oct. 15th, 1847. Joshua Orne, 62 years.
June, 1796. Hon. Azor Orne, 65 years.

The above are all the entries on the Record up to 1850.

The following in relation to births, marriages and deaths from 1675 to 1840 has been received from the city clerk of Lynn :—

Timothy Orne and Rebecca Taylor were married in 1747.

Rebecca, daughter of Simond and Mary Orne, born 1730.

Lois Orne, born 1768.

*Eunice, born 1771.

Bridget, born 1774, children of John and Bridget Orne.

The following is from the history of Framingham :

Submit Horn married Moses Haven, September 17, 1794.

Robert, Jun. married in Southb. Thankful Moore, Nov. 1, 1749, and was father of Elizabeth born Aug. 28, 1750, m. Moses Newton 1772.

---

*Eunice Orne married Dec. 23, 1796, Aaron Green of the fifth generation in descent from James Green who settled in Charlestown 1634.
  Bourne's History of Wells and Kennebunk says that Eunice Orne of Lynnfield (Lynn) Mass., was married to Benjamin Brown Nov., 1795. Benjamin Brown came to Kennebunk in 1782.

Samuel b. 1753.

Robert b. 1754.

Catherine b. 1757, m. Jedidiah Parker and died 1823.

Robert was son of Robert of Marlb., who m. Elizabeth Maynard, 1723, and had Robert, b. August 6, 1726; Robert[sen] died in Southb. in 1760 or 1763 ; his widow, Elizabeth died 1766. John was early of Salem and took the freeman's oath May 18, 1631.

From this record it would seem that the Horne family of Southboro, Mass., traced its ancestry to John Orne (Horne) of Salem (1630). Another evidence that Horn and Orne are the same name in this family is from the fact that Samuel Horn, a prominent citizen of Lowell, Mass., is of the Southboro Horn family, and is the son of Windsor and Matilda (Nicholas) Horn. He was born in Southboro, Dec. 31, 1806. See history of Middlesex Co., Mass., Vol II., p. 108.

According to an old pedigree, Samuel Horne, rector of Otham, in the County of Kent, died August 16, 1768. He married Anne Hendley, who died March 10, 1787. Anne was the great granddaughter of Sir Thomas Hendley of Corshorne, Co. of Kent, living 1619 ; sherif of Kent, 1616 or 1638. He married Elizabeth da. of John Wilford of Enfield, Esq.

(Anne[4], Boyer[3] Hendley, Esq., John and Sir Thomas[1] Hendley). The earliest record we have of the Hendley family of Courshorne is that of Thomas Hendley, Esq., brother of Sir Walter ob. 1590 ; Sir Walter Hendley of Coursehorne Knt. ob. 6 Edward VI. 1552.

Arms-Quarterly, 1st and 4th gu. a fesse vair, for Horne.

2[d] and 3[d]—Paly, bendy, gu. and az., eight martlets, in orle, or, for Hendley.

Crest of Horne.—an owl ppr.

Crest of Hendley.—A martlet or.

According to another old pedigree in the author's possession, there was a Godfrey Alchorne of Uckfield, Co. Sussex, Visitation of Kent, 1619. He had numerous descendants. Alchorne is undoubtedly an old spelling for Elkhorne, for this family had for

Arms.—A buck's head, cabossed, sa. a chief, indented, of the second.

Crest.—A human heart gu. ducally crowned or, betw. a pair of wings ar.

Quarterings in Visitation 1619.

1. Paly of six, ar. ar.d sa. a fesse gu. charged with a fleur-de-lis for difference, for Walsingham.

2. Vert, a lion, rampant, guardant, ar. for Love.

3. Sa. three rams' heads. cabossed, ar. horned or, for Ram.

Samuel Horne had two sons, viz., William Horne, rector of Otham, ob. July 10, 1821, aet. 81. He m. Elizabeth, bo. 1st March, 1738, ob. 4th June, 1774. George Horne, D. D., Bishop of Norwich; he m. Felicia, da. of Burton, Esq., of Leicestershire. William Horne had son William, clerk of Gore-court, rector of Otham, living 1828; he m. Maria, da. of the Rev. William Whitear, rector of Oare, Co. Sussex, m. 1799.

George Horne, D. D., had Felicia, who m. the Rev. Silby Hele; Maria unmarried; Sarah, who mar. the Rev. ——— Hole.

The parish of Coursehorne, or Corshorne, was so named in all probability on account of its fine opportunities for the pursuit of game. Dryden's phrase, "With horns and hounds," when applied in a description of what there was formerly commonly observed, would not be deemed inapt.

An owl proper for the crest of Horne, like the three rams' heads, cabossed ar. horned or, for Ram, suggests the idea that names sometimes have their origin in the ensigns armorial of families. The owl proper or horned for the crest in a helmet, conveys to the mind the conception of strength, no less than that of ornament.

As an important mark of personal prowess the surname Horne shorn of its initial " H," for the sake of euphony or with a pretension that the family descended from the Huguenots, or from the French, is meaningless, for as already intimated, the name " Orne " is not found in the lists of the old Celtic warriors or of other valorous knights. Ornus in Latin signified the wild mountain ash, and also a lance; no one thus far has ventured to assert that " Orne " is a derivative of " Ornus," and no one who has borne the name " Orne " as a part of a Christian name has Latinized it as Ornus in a college catalogue. The name " Orne " as Horne stands as

indeclinable.   The statement, made in the edition of 1845, of Mrs.
Lincoln's Botany, that Ornus, an ash, is from the Hebrew is
erroneous.   The Hebrew word, אָרָן aran, occurring in
Isaiah, chapter 44, v. 14, signifies pinus cedrus, the cedar of
Lebanon; the tree was formerly very abundant on Mount
Lebanon. The wood is odoriferous, and was much used in the
temple and the royal palace for ornamental work.   For a name
אָרָן aran has no significance.

The Latin word Ornus is in the feminine gender, and was
therefore not suitable in the earlier ages for a strong surname.

An instance of a proper name's receiving an initial "H" is that
of "Holborn," which was one of the neighboring hamlets in the
district about London, England, in 1077, and which consisted of
only a few houses on the banks of the "Old bourn," a stream
which ran into Fleet river, called "Holborn."

Other names are occasionally met with that are spelled with or
without the initial "H," as "Horton," "Orton," "Hoare," "Oare
or "Ore," "Hyde," "Ide," and the like.   Some of the names of
these different spellings have had a common origin, while others
are not related.   The Italian for our English word "hostile" is
"ostile," for "host" is "oste."   It should be remarked that "H"
is never sounded in Italian. So also the ע and א, letters peculiar
to the organs of the Shemitish race, have an initial sound of "g,"
slightly rattled in the throat, and in uttering those sounds, the
mouth must be more open than when pronouncing our English
vowels.   It is the prevailing usage for Europeans and Americans
at present to pass over ע and א in reading the language, and to
write the words with the Roman or occidental letters.   Scholars
in their endeavor to sound these letters with only an initial
spiritus lene, find that the initial spiritus asper is often furtively
brought out.

Some of our forefathers having been associated so much with
the people of Holland, that were accustomed to pronounce certain
letters of the alphabet with the rough breathing, found it not
unwise to modify this habit by omitting or changing in the writing of their names at a later period some of the rougher conson-

ants. Many words which we write with an initial "H," in Chaucer's time were written without the "H," as "Ector" for "Hector" and "Ipolita" for "Hippolita," while others which at that period began with "H" no longer have that letter. The unsettled state of the English language during Chaucer's time (1340–1400) left its impress on the habits of the people. Chaucer had a special fondness for the Italian popular writers; this was undoubtedly enhanced by his embassy and residence in Genoa. In his own vernacular he made numberless changes which contributed to the growth and development among the people of the methods of the Italian school. Skeat* in speaking of the pronunciation of Chaucer's dialect says "h" initial=h, just as at present; he says the pronunciation of it seems to have been generally omitted in unaccented words as he, his, him, hire=her, hire =their, hem=them, and often in hath, hadde, haue, just as we still have "I've told 'em;" and in some French words, as "host," "honour," "honest," etc., it was probably omitted as at present. It will be observed that in the name of John Horn, Horn would . be unaccented. The accent or the distinguishing element would be on "John" as Joh'n Horn=John Orne or John-nOrne. Joseph Horn=Joseph-phOrne. Jonathan Horn=Jonathan-nOrne. This pronunciation would be after the style of the Norman French.

As the early settlers lapsed into the habit of spelling or of writing their names as they were sounded, the employment of certain letters appeared to be useless; consequently they were omitted. The signing of the name of John Orne in the form that it was to so important a document as a last will and testament would not at that time be considered an illegal or an unnatural act. The fusion of the Norman and the Saxon nations also made many modifications. French was the prevailing language at Court. Those who affected to be learned or to belong to the higher classes did not hesitate to show this by a resort to manners that savored of Norman French or of the post Latin races.

The name of William Horn at Dover did not suffer through

---

* Introduction to Chaucer's Canterbury Tales, page xiv. Oxford edition, by Rev. Walter W. Skeat, Litt. D., L.L.D., 1891.

the influences left by the Norman incursion, but retained its full Saxon spelling. Hume makes mention of a curious instance of a Norman name that received the initial aspirate "H." Hume says that Robert, duke of Normandy, the sixth in descent from Rollo, when riding out one day through the town of Falaise, espied a certain damsel of mean condition, a skinner's daughter, dancing with others near the wayside. The form and comely carriage of her body, the natural beauty and graces of her countenance, the simplicity of her rural birth, her behavior and attire, pleased the duke. That night he had her procured at his lodgings; she in due time bore him a son, who became no other than William the Conqueror. Some say that Robert made her his wife. Her name was Arlotte. The English afterward adding an aspirate to her name (according as the author says was their natural manner of pronouncing) termed her a "Harlot," as they do every woman who may have been indiscreet.

(See the Harleian Miscellany, 1793, on the life of King William the First, Surnamed the Conqueror).

According to the Wentworth Gen. Vol. 1. pp. 398-400, 454-6; vol. II. pp. 206-9, Mary[4], daughter of Samuel[3] and Patience (Downs) Wentworth, b. 14 September, 1757, m. 19 March, 1777, Andrew Horne, Jr., son of Andrew of Somersworth, N. H., and grandson of William Horne of Dover, N. H. He was a soldier of the Revolution. They lived at Great Falls, N. H. She died 4th July, 1814.

Patience[5] Horne, b. 5 January, 1782, m. 10 March, 1803, James Dore, born 27 August, 1782. She remembered being present at the funeral of her grandfather, Samuel[3] Wentworth. Wentworth[5] Horn m. Ruth Jones and died, having had thirteen children :——

1.   Ruth[6] Horne, m. Bumford.
2.   Andrew[6] Horne, m. Louisa Lord.
3.   Mary[6] Horne, m. Oliver[7] Wentworth.
4.   Thomas[6] Horne, m. Sally York, of Newfield, Maine.
5.   Veranus Horne, m. Mary Hodgdon before he was of age ; his wife having paid $210 "for his time."
6.   Thayos[6] Horne, m. Edmund Lord of Berwick, Maine.

7. James[6] Horne.

8. Edwin Horne.

9. Seth[6] Wentworth Horne.

10. Sylvina[6] Horne, b. 21 April, 1839 ; m. 10 Sept. ,1857, James W. Chapman of Boston, Mass., where they lived.

11. Wentworth[6] Horne lived at Great Falls in 1875.

Andrew[5] Horne.

Mary[5] Horne.

Betsey[5] Horne, m. Amaziah Lord.

Sarah[5] Baker, b. 8 June, 1755, m. Ichabod Horne of Dover, N. H., (of whom see below).

Daniel Horne, b. in 1689. His grandson, Michael Read, who lately died in Dover at an advanced age, and who kept accurate records, said that this Daniel[1] Horne was a native of Scotland, as already mentioned. He died in Dover 7 April, 1777. He had wife Mary, who was baptized in Dover, with her son Daniel Horne, 28 September, 1718. She had :

1. Daniel[2] Horne, b, 23 October, 1716 (of whom see below).

2. Ichabod[2] Horne, b. 5 March, 1720-1.

3. Mary[2] Horne, b. 13 April, 1724.

4. Benjamin[2] Horne, b. 11 January, 1725-6.

5. Paul[2] Horne, b. 24 May, 1730.

6. Abigail[2] Horne, b. 28 March, 1734.

Daniel[2] Horne, son of Daniel[1] as above, lived in Dover ; m. Lydia, daughter of Joseph and Elizabeth Roberts and widow of Samuel Ham.

Daniel[2] and Lydia (Roberts) Horne had :

1. Abigail[3] Horne, baptised 2 October, 1743, m. 31 Dec. 1770, Thomas Watson.

2. Ichabod[3] Horne, baptised 6 October, 1745; m. Sarah Baker, as above.

3. Paul[3] Horne, baptised 3 July, 1748 ; m. 27 October, 1774, Hannah, daughter of Dr. Cheney.

4. Betsey[3] Horne, baptised 9 August, 1752 ; m. second wife Clement Ham.

5. Mary[3] Horne, baptised 13 October, 1754 ; m. 12 March, 1776, Win   p Watson.

6. Deborah[3] Horne, baptised 31 October, 1756; m. 8 March, 1778, Michael Reed. He was born in Kilkenny, Ireland, 1741; emigrated, settled in Dover. N. H.; died 28 Jan., 1812.

Sarah[5] Baker, b. 8 June, 1775; m. Ichabod Horne. They lived on the Tole-end road in Dover, N. H.; his half-sister Lydia, daughter of his mother by a prior marriage to Samuel Horne, m. Ephraim[4] (1761-2) Horne.

Ichabod and Sarah[5] (Baker) Horne had twenty-two children, ten of whom died in infancy. She died March, 1825. Their surviving children were:

1. Lydia[6] Horne, b. 11 Jan., 1773; m. 22 July, 1807, Captain Twoombly, a revolutionary soldier.

2. Elizabeth[6] Horne, died aged 2 years.

3. Nancy[6] Horne, b. April, 1777; m. James Kimball, and died Feb., 1849.

4. Sally[6] Horne, twin with Nancy[6], died of consumption aged 21 years.

5. Daniel[6] Horne, b. March, 1779; m. Sarah Watson, had two sons, and died April, 1850.

6. Mehetabel[6] Horne, m. Joshua Ham; she died in 1825, and he m. 2nd her sister, Susanna[6] Horne.

7. Otis Horne[6], b. 1784; lived in Dover.

8. Samuel[6] Horne lived in Haverhill, Mass.; m. and had four daughters, all married.

9. Gershom[6] Horne, m. Eleanor Horne, and died without issue.

10. Elizabeth[6] Horne, m. 1815, Aaron Watson.

11. Susanna[6] Horne, b. in 1795; m. 22 Sept., 1825 (second wife), Joshua Horne (as above).

12. Thomas[6] Horne, m. daughter of Joseph[7] and Betsey (Watson) Waldron.

[Lydia, daughter of Isaac Horne, was m. to James Chesley. He was then seventy years of age; she was twenty-two.

Peter Horne was the son of William Horne, m. Mercy[5], died in Rochester, N. H.

Peter[5] and Mercy[5] (Wentworth) Horne had: —

1. Jacob[6] Horne, m. and lived in Wolfborough, N. H.

2. Edmund[6] Horne, m. and lived in Brookfield, N. H.

3. Elijah[6] Horne, m. and lived in Milton, N. H.]

Lydia Roberts m. Gershom Horne of Somersworth, N. H., son of Andrew Horne, who was son of William Horne of Dover.

William Horne, as said before, was first taxed at Cocheco, Dover, in 1659. He is doubtless the William Horne who was earlier at Salisbury, Mass.; deeds of Salisbury lands being on record. He bought of Elder Starbuok of Dover, 20 Sept., 1661, two hundred and forty acres between Cocheco and Tole-end in Dover, parts of which were recently in the posession of his lineal descendants. He was killed in the massacre by the Indians, 28 June, 1689. He had wife Elizabeth and children as before mentioned.

William[2] Horne is said, however, by Wentworth to have had:—

1. Thomas[3] Horne, who, as "only son, quitclaimed land to Cousin John[3] Horne," b. January 1717-18.

2. Elizabeth[3] Horne, m. Moses Kimmin.

John Evans of Dover and wife Elizabeth[4], daughter of Moses and Elizabeth[3] Kimmin, and "granddaughter of William[2] Horne, 10 Aug., 1749, for £62 quitclaimed to John Horne all her right by heirship by our mother Elizabeth Kimmin."

Thomas[2] Horne, b. 28 Nov., 1676, was of Dover. He m. 1st, 14 April, 1699, Judith, daughter of Geo. and Eleanor (Evans) Ricker, b. 1 Feb., 1681.

Thomas[2] Horne had by wife Judith (Ricker) : —

1. Sarah[3] Horne, b. 14 Jan., 1699-1700.
2. Ichabod[3] Horne, b. 7 Nov., 1702.
3. Thomas[3] Horne, b. 23 Oct., 1705.
4. William[3] Horne, b. 25 June, 1710.

The, Thomas Horne (perhaps this Thomas[2]), who had wife Esther, had :

1. Judith Horne, b. 16 August, 1720.
2. Margaret Horne, b. 16 April, 1722.
3. Samuel Horne, b. 16 Feb., 1724.
4. Abigail Horne, b. 7 Dec., 1725.
5. Drusilla Horne, b. 18 June, 1727.

Margaret[2] Horne, b. 10 May, 1679 ; died in 1697.

Mercy[2] Horne, m. 6 April, 1704.

Mercy[2] Horne, Joseph Evans' wife, "daughter of William Horne," 1 Dec., 1748, conveyed to "John[3] Horne, grandson of William[1] Horne," all her right in land which her father purchased of Elder Starbuck in 1661. Their great granddaughter, Hannah Evans, m. Lorenzo[6] Rollins.

John[2] Horne, son of William[1], as above, was of Dover. He m. 30 June, 1686, Mary, daughter of John and Mary (Heard) Ham, b. 2 Oct., 1668. He died March, 1696-7, and she m. 2nd 29 August, 1698, John Waldron, and was mother of Mehetabel Waldron who married James[4] Chesley; and grandmother of Col. John Waldron, who m. (third wife) Margaret (Frost), widow of Hon. John[5] Wentworth, Jr. John[2] Horne had (probably others also) :

1. John[3] Horne of Dover, who, as "eldest son and rightful heir," acknowledged 31 Oct., 1717, receipt of 60 acres in Dover from "Uncle" Thomas[2] Horne as "full proportion due" his father John[2] Horne, out of estate of William[1] Horne. He m. 29 Dec., 1728, Elizabeth Heard. By deeds he appears to have had :

1. Nathaniel[4] Horne, to whom his father conveyed land of January, 1734-5. He m. Sarah, daughter of Ichabod and Abigail Hayes, b. 30 Dec., 1716. Baptisms of three daughters of Nathaniel[4] Horne are on Dover church records.

2. Isaac[4] Horne, to whom his father gave the homestead 14 Dec., 1749, recorded 18 March, 1773. He is doubtless the Isaac Horne whose daughter Lydia Horne (second wife) m. James Chesley.

3. William[4] Horne, who quitclaimed to John Horne, 21 Feb., 1754, all right in his (William[4]) father, John's[3] estate.

4. John[4] Horne.

2. William[3] Horne, probably. He gave receipt in full for £20 to John[3] Horne, 17 July, 1731. Thomas Horne, witness. He conveyed this land, with dwelling house then on it, to son Ebenezer Horne and Mary, his wife, 26 Feb., 1754. The same date he conveyed to son William[3d] land in Somersworth, N. H., on which said son William then lived, (A William Horne, apparently not this one, then a "friend," m. 9 September, 1713, Mary Varney and had daughter Sarah Horne, b. 1 Aug., 1714, who m. (1st), 31 July, 1734, Isaac Hanson, (2d), 2 Jan., 1760, Thomas Tuttle, and died in 1812.)

William[3] Horne made will 14 Dec., 1767, proved 29 August, 1770, mentioning wife Elizabeth (from some language apparently a second wife) and eleven children. The married daughters' names are given in the will as follows : —

1. Ebenezer[4] Horne, who had wife Mary; he "gentleman" of Dover, conveyed to Moses Horne, 17 Oct., 1777, the land which his father bought of John Horne in 1772, with two other places, excepting three acres he had given to his son William[5] Horne. The baptisms of five sons and two daughters are on Dover church records, including Stephen Wentworth[6] Horne, who was the youngest of five children, baptised 31 Oct., 1756; he was collector of Wolfborough, N. H., in 1791.

2. Andrew[4] Horne, was of Dover, N. H. He had probably, with others :

1. Andrew[5] Horne of Somersworth, N. H., who m. Mary[4] Wentworth.

2. Jacob[5] Horne, never married. By will dated 1 Oct., 1808, proved 29 Nov., 1808, he left all his property to nephew Jacob[6] Horne, son of Gershom[5] Horne.

3. Gershom[5] Horne, m. Lydia, da. of Col. James and Martha (Woodsum) Roberts. Besides sons James[6] Horne, Charles[6] Horne and Isaac[6] Horne, he had : —

1. Jacob[6] Horne, m. his mother's cousin Esther Heard, as in above note.

2. Gershom[6] Horne, b. 4 Dec., 1803, m. 14 Sept., 1830, Abigail K. Wentworth.

3. John[6] Horne, m. 4 January, 1827, his cousin, Ruth[6] Wentworth.

4. Ephraim[5] Horne, m. Mary Wentworth; their son John[6] Horne m. 3 March, 1835, Martha[6] Wentworth.

3. William[4] Horne, was of Somersworth, N. H.

4. Peter[4] Horne, blacksmith, received from his father, 26 Feb., 1754, land in Rochester, N. H., and lived there. He m. Mercy[5] Wentworth. His inventory, entered 19 Sept., 1795, including eight acres in Rochester, N. H. "drawn to the original right of William Horne." The dower of his widow Mercy[5] was set off 14 Nov., 1800. "Rebecca, daughter of Peter Horne of

Rochester," (doubtless this Peter) m. 20 Oct., 1783, John[5] Wentworth.

Peter Horne of Rochester, who m. 28 Feb., 1793, Eunice[6] Wentworth, is said to have been his son.

5. Moses[4] Horne, lived in Rochester, N. H., on land joining his brother Peter's[4]; was dead before 1800. Guardians were appointed to four children under the age of fourteen.

   6. Sarah[4] Horne, m. —— Gould.

   7. Mary[4] Horne, living at date of her father's will.

   8. Lydia[4] Horne, m. Twombly.

   9. Mercy[4] Horne, m. Hussey.

  10. Abigail[4] Horne, m. Hayes.

  11. Martha Horne, m. —— Copp. (See Wentworth Gen.)

The name of Orne in N. H. appears to have been derived from that of Horne. In 1807, Isaiah Horne* (Isaiah[5], Ebenezer[4], William[3], John[2], William[1]), and family were named Orne by special act of the N. H. Legislature (see vol. 16. p. 405). Others also in N. H., after that date, changed Horne to Orne — thus Albert W. Horne of Wolfborough was changed to Albert W. Orne by N. H. Special Law in 1828 (see vol. 25, p. 71).

Nathaniel Horne, of Wolfborough, was named Augustine Woodbridge Orne in 1828 (see vol. 25, p. 71).

David Ambrose Horne was named David Ambrose Orne in 1848 (see vol. 38, p. 35, N. H. Laws).

By Act 1829, Chap. 17, Massachusetts Special Laws, the name of Benjamin Crosby Horne of Gloucester was changed to Benjamin Crosby Orne.

1771, Feb. 28, an Ebenezer Horne of Rochester, N. H., and Rebecca Pinkham of Dover were married.

The town Records of Corinth, Vermont, show that the names of the children of Joseph[6] Horne (Joseph[6], Joseph[5], Joseph[4], William[3], Joseph[2], William[1]), who was there as early as 1794 were entered as Orne. The father of Joseph had, as will be remarked, served as a revolutionary soldier and had kept his name without change from Joseph Horn. The voluntary change in the names

---

* Mercy, William, Betsey, Ebenezer, and Stephen Wentworth Horne were baptized at Dover, 31 Oct., 1756. Isaiah Horne, son of Ebenezer Horne, was baptized in Dover, 15 July, 1759. Jeremiah, son of Ebenezer Horne, was baptized 9 January, 1769.

appears to have been somewhat allowed in Vermont until it became necessary in 1863 to pass a statute giving authority for such change in name. The following is the act: —

How persons may change their names.

Section 1. Any person of full age and sound mind, other than a married woman, who may wish to alter his name, may make an instrument in writing under his hand and seal, attested by three credible witnesses, and acknowledged before the judge of probate in the district where such person resides, therein declaring such intention, designating the name he wishes to assume, and shall cause the same to be recorded in the records of said probate court, and in the clerk's office in the town in which said person resides, which being done, such person shall thereafter be known and called by the name designated in said instrument.

Section 2. This act shall take effect from its passage. Approved, Oct. 30, 1863.

When John Horne of Salem died in 1680, leaving a will which he had signed as John Orne, there seemed to have been no questions raised; he had, however, been a prominent man, and slight difference in the spelling of names was not unfrequent.

The statement that Daniel Horne was a native of Scotland was undoubtedly made from tradition held by some of the Horne families during Michael Read's time, but it should not be received as authoritative regarding the place of his nativity. It will be observed that Mr. Read failed to designate the name of a Scottish parish from which he could have emigrated. It will also be seen that Daniel Horne died in Dover, 7 April, 1777, and that Mr. Read did not become connected with the Horne family until 8 March, 1778, the time of his marriage to Deborah Horne. It is therefore not reasonable to suppose that he would until after that time have taken a special interest in the genealogical history of that family. Daniel Horne, as said before, was born in 1689, and was undoubtedly a son or a descendant of William Horne of Dover. Mr. Charles W. Tibbets, a gentleman familiar with the early records of Dover, informed me recently by letter that the record of births and deaths in New Hampshire was not kept as in Massachusetts; he further says there is a record of only about two hundred marriages prior to 1800. He says that it seems the Horne family did not bring their family records to be recorded. From all accounts it seems that the Horne family came from St. James, Clerkenwell, London.

The name of this parish originated from an ancient well, round which the parish clerks of London were in the habit of assembling at certain hours, for the performance of sacred dramas, noticed in the reign of Henry II. by Fitz-Stephen under the appellation of Fons Clericorum. The parish is not mentioned in the Domesday-book, being probably at the time of the survey an undistinguished portion of the great forest of Middlesex. The site appears to have been well adapted to the celebration of those sacred festivals, for which it was selected from being in the centre of gently rising grounds, which form an extensive and natural amphitheatre for the accommodation of the numerous spectators who attended on such occasions. The most celebrated of these festivals took place in 1391, in the reign of Richard II., and continued for three days, during which several sacred dramas were performed by the clerks in presence of the king and queen, attended by the whole court. About the year 1100, Sir Jordan Brisset and his wife founded a priory here for nuns of the Benedictine Order, dedicated to St· Mary, site being now occupied by the parish church of St. James; the revenue at the dissolution was £282.16.5. The same Jordan founded also an hospital for Knights Hospitallers of the Order of St. John of Jerusalem, which was liberally endowed with lands and with other gifts.

The establishment of these monasteries naturally drew around them a number of dependent dwellings, but the parish made little progress in the number of its inhabitants prior to the time of Elizabeth, in whose reign, with the exception of some "banqueting houses and summer houses," it contained only a few straggling cottages, and some good houses in the immediate neighborhood of the religious house; its increase was afterward more rapid, and in 1619, during the time of the residence there of John Horne, the father of the first John Horne (Orne) of Salem, and of the first William Horne of Dover, several nobleman and gentlemen were numbered among its inhabitants. Since then the construction of more pleasant streets and well built houses, and the more recent laying out of the Spa-fields and its neighborhood, have rendered this one of its most popular resorts in the vicinity of the great metropolis.

There are slight vestiges of the Fons Clericorum or Clerken-well, on the site of which the houses in the close have been built, consisting chiefly of a pump over which is an inscription. Clerken-well manor, formerly denominated the manor of St. John of Jeru-salem, includes several out-portions of the parishes of St. Sepulchre, St. Luke (Old shire), and Hornsey with those parts of the parish of Clerkenwell called the liberties of Cold Bath Fields, St. John of Jerusalem, Clerkenwell Close, Wood Close, and Pentonville. This district was formerly called the parish of St. James Clerken-well, and the church of St. James was the only church within it; it is now divided into two districts, one called St. James's, and the other St. John's, both in the archdeaconry and diocese of London. Among the distinguished natives and residents of Clerkenwell may be mentioned Sir Thomas Chaloner, Bishop Burnet, Sir John Oldcastle, Baron Cobham, and Edward Cave, who established the " Gentleman's Magazine," and whose printing-office was over St. John's Gate. (For this account of Clerkenwell, see S. Lewis's Topographical Dictionary of London.)

This large district and out-parish of the City of London still has an imposing Session-house, green Prison-house and New River Head-water Reservoir (or Head-water cistern, as the English term it), for the supply of water to the great metropolis. "St. John's Gate" is the only vestige of the ancient priory that was erected in that locality. During my visit to Clerkenwell in 1890, I found many objects there that would be of interest to the tourist.

Samuel Metcalf, born in Rutland, Mass., in 1739, died in 1785, married Hannah Richardson of Leicester, Mass. She was born there in 1743 and was the youngest of three daughters of Thomas Richardson of Rutland, Mass., by his wife, Jane Downing*. The other daughters were Lucy, b. in Leicester, 1740, and Elizabeth,

---

*Daughter of Captain Nathaniel Downing of Ipswich and his wife, Margaret Pynchon : the record of their illustrious ancestors is given on subsequent pages.

b. in Leicester, 1741 ; m. Nathan Lamb of Spencer. Mr. Thomas
Richardson, the father, came from Malden, and had by his first
wife, Elizabeth,——Elizabeth, b. 1729 ; Samuel, b. 1722 ; James,
b. 1723 ; Philip, b. 1725 ; Mary, b. 1729; Rebecca, b. 1731 ; m.
James Smith of Leicester, 1751. All Mr. Richardson's children
by 1st wife were born in Leicester. James Richardson moved out
of Leicester in 1777. Thomas Richardson, the father, lived in
what was the Baptist Parsonage House. His son commanded a
company of men in Col. Ruggles' regiment at Fort William
Henry in August, 1756.

The children of Samuel[6] Metcalf and his wife Hannah (Rich-
ardson) were Ebenezer, David, Thomas, Esther, Samuel, John,
Joseph, Jane, b. July 30, 1776, (died in Bristol, R. I., March, 1860),
Elizabeth, Hannah, Alpha, and Abigail. Jane m. Joseph[9] Orne
(Horne) Nov., 1793. Samuel[6] was son of Ebenezer[5] Metcalf of
Rutland, b. Jan. 8, 1691, died 1751 (m. July 11, 1732, Margaret[4]
Rockwood, b. Sept. 4, 1699. She was the daughter of Nathaniel[3]
Rockwood, of Holliston, Mass., deacon, b. Feb. 23, 1665, died Sept.
24, 1721 at Wrentham), m. Dec. 7, 1698, Joanna Ellis, b. Jan. 17,
1677, daughter of Thomas Ellis of Medfield, by wife, Mary Wight,
m. 1657, settled in Wrentham, and had :—

1. Margaret[4], b. Sept. 4, 1699; m. Ebenezer Metcalf, July 11,
1732.
2. Nathaniel[4].
3. Benjamin[4].
4. Abigail[4].
5. Ebenezer[4].

Nathaniel[3] Rockwood was son of Nicholas[2], first located in
Braintree, and had wives, Jane, Margaret Holbrook, and Silence
Duntling; 1650 removed to Medfield ; had :—
Samuel[3].
Benjamin[3].
Josiah[3].
Elizabeth[3].
Joseph[3].
Nathaniel[3].
Nicholas[2] Rockwood was son of Richard[1] of Braintree, who m.

Agnes. Rockwood and Rocket were formerly the same name, meaning rocky wood. John Rocket, planter, was in Dorchester, Mass., 1633. This family is one that is found in Dorset and Suffolk counties, England. (See Genealogies of Holliston.)

Ebenezer[5] Metcalf was an early and respectable settler in Rutland; he bought land and lived west of Ball's Spring. He and his wife Margaret had children as follows: —

Ebenezer[6], b. in 1734.
Seth[6], b. in 1736.
Esther[6], b. 1737.
Samuel[6], b. 1739.
Mary[6], b. 1741-2.
(See history of Ruthland, Mass.)

Ebenezer[5] was son of Eleazar[4] Metcalf of Wrentham, Mass., b. in Dedham, Mass., March 20, 1653, d. in Wrentham, May 14, 1704; deacon; m. April 9, 1684, Melatiah Fisher, and had ten children:

Eleazar[5], b. May 30, 1685.
Michael[5], b. Jan. 25, 1687.
Samuel[5], b. Jan. 15, 1689.
Ebenezer[5], b. Jan. 8, 1691.
Jonathan[5], b. April 9, 1693.
Melatiah[5], b. April 29, 1695.
Timothy[5], b. July 2, 1697.
Martha[5] and Mary[5], b. Aug. 27, 1699.
Eleazar[5], b. Nov. 21, 1700-1.

Eleazar[4] Metcalf was son of Michael[3] Metcalf, b. in Norwich, England, Aug. 29, 1620, d. Dec. 27, 1664, and admitted a freeman by Mass. Gen. Court, May 13, 1642; m. April 21, 1644, Mary, daughter of John Fairbanks, and had seven children:

Michael[4], b. Jan. 21, 1645.
Jonathan[4], b. Sept. 10, 1650.
Eleazar[4], b. March 20, 1653.
Sarah[4], b. Jan. 7, 1656.
Mary[4], b. Aug. 15, 1659.

Michael[3] was son of Michael[2] Metcalf, b. in Tatterford, England, June 17, 1586. "Dornix Weaver," in Norwich, England, came to

America to escape religious persecutions, after losing his property
by a Star Chamber fine; m. Oct. 13, 1616, Sarah, b. in Waynham,
Eng., June 17, 1593. (See American Ancestry, vol. 7.)

To show how Michael Metcalf came to America, the following
record is taken from Mr. John Camden Hotten's work, which was
gleaned by him from the State Paper department in England,
and which has recently been published in London: —

"Register of persons about to pass into foreign parts,
1637. These people went to New England with William :*
Andros: of Ipswich M^r of the: John: and Dorothy: of Ipswich
and with William Andrewes his son M^r of the Rose : of Yarmouth.

　　　*　　　*　　　*　　　*　　　*　　　*　　　*

April the 18th 1637. The examination of Michill: Metcalfe: of
No'wich Do'nix Weauear|aged, 45 years with|8 children|Michill :
Thomas: Mary: Sarah: Elizabeth: Martha: Jonii and Rebecca:
and his saruant Thomas Comberbach: aged|16|years ar desirous
to pass to boston in New England to inhabit.| | |"

Mr. Tilden in his Hist. of Medfield, 1887, p. 436 says, that
Michael Metcalf was a "dornik weaver" and that he fled to this
country from persecutions which he gives in Michael Metcalf's
own words: "I was forced, for the sake of the liberty of my
conscience, to flee from my wife and children, and go into New
England; taking ship for the voyage, Sept. 17, 1636, being by
tempests tossed up and down the seas till the Christmas following,
then veering about to Plymouth in Old England in which time I
met with many sore afflictions. Leaving the ship, I went down to
Yarmouth in Norfolk county, whence I shipped myself and family
to come to New England, sailed April 15, 1637, and arrived three
days before midsummer following, with my wife and nine children,
and a servant." In a postscript, says Mr. Tilden, Michael Metcalf
alludes again to troubles he sustained at the hands of Bishop Wren
and the chancellor, in consequence of which he was driven from
his family: "Sometimes my wife did hide me in the roof of the
house, covering me with straw." John Metcalf was a son of Mich-

---

* Mr. Hotten has fortunately preserved the very peculiar punctuation of the
sailing list.

ael, and was born in Norwich, England, in 1622; his boyhood was spent among scenes like these. The family settled at Dedham, Mass.; John, m. in 1647, Mary Chickering. John removed to Medfield about 1652, with his wife and three children. He served on the board of selectmen six years, and had the title of commissioner in 1682. He died in 1690; his wife in 1698. children : —

John, b. 1648.

Michael, b. 1650.

Elizabeth ; m. Joseph Ellis.

Joseph, b. 1658.

Experience, 1661-1730 ; m. Isaac Wheeler, whose daughter, Experience Wheeler, m. Joseph[4] Clarke, as above stated.

Hannah, 1664-1719; m. in 1683, Elisha Bullen.

Mary, 1668-1727 ; m. in 1687, Eleazar Ellis (See op. cit.).

Samuel[6] Metcalf (Ebenezer[5], Eleazar[4], Michael[3], Michael[2], Leonard[1]), who m. Hannah Richardson and had by her the twelve children as above named, and who died in 1785, had a good military record. His name appears as private in Captain John Boyd's company, Col. Greaton's regt. Lexington Alarm, April 19, 1775 ; he belonged to Wrentham, Mass., service eight days ; next he was in Captain Boyd's co., Col. Heath's regt. ; he was from Wrentham, enlisted April 27, 1775. The muster roll was made out, and dated Oct. 5, 1775. His name appears on an order and bounty roll for coat or its equivalent for eight months' service in 1775 in Capt. Boyd's co. Col. John Greaton's regiment. Dated Cambridge, Dec. 23, 1775. Return of men enlisted into the Continental army from John Metcalf's North company, dated Wrentham, Feb. 16, 1775, belonged to Wrentham, expiration of enlistment.

Samuel Metcalf appears with the rank of sergeant on Continental Army Pay Accounts of Captain Daniel's co., Col. Nixon's regt., for service from Feb. 14, 1777, to Dec. 31, 1779. He is credited to the town of Franklin Residence, Franklin.

Reported 31 months and 16 days service as sergeant and three months as private. [It should be remarked that Franklin, March 2, 1778, was incorporated as a town and was set off from the westerly part of Wrentham]. Samuel Metcalf appears as private in Continental A. P. account of Captain Daniel's co., Col. Nixon's regt., service from Jan. 1, 1780, to Feb. 14, 1780. Residence at this time in Wrentham. Was not credited in this short service to the new town. Feb. 15, 1780, Samuel Metcalf appears in Joseph Daniel's company, Col. Nixon's regt. Samuel Metcalf appears in a list of men mustered in Suffolk county in Captain Daniel's co., Col. Nixon's regt.; return made by Nathaniel Barton. Dated Boston, May 11, 1779 — 3 years.

Samuel Metcalf appears on a certificate of service dated and given by Brig. Gen. John Nixon for service as sergeant in Col. Nixon's regiment, in camp, from or before August 15, 1777, to time of granting certificate. Allowed in Council, April 1, 1779. Sergeant in Captain Daniel's co., 6th regiment, for service June 1, to July, 1779.

Samuel Metcalf appears in a list of officers of the Mass. Militia as lieutenant, commanded July 10, 1780; detached from Suffolk county to be tranferred to Continental army by Resolve of June 22, 1779, 3 months' service.

Samuel Metcalf appears as lieutenant on muster and pay roll of Captain Nathan Thayer's co., Col. Ebenezer Thayer's regt., enlisted July 10, 1780, discharged Oct. 9th, 1780. Service 3 mos., 10 days. Stationed at West Point 3 mos. service, 10 days' travel included. Suffolk co. regt., raised to reinforce Con[l]. Army. Samuel Metcalf appears on a return of men raised under Resolve of Dec. 2, 1780. Raised May 31, 1781; term of enlistment 3 years. Belonged to Franklin, county of Suffolk.

Samuel Metcalf of Franklin appears on a roll service 3 years in the Continental Army dated at Franklin, April 16, 1781. Samuel Metcalf appears on a roll as lieutenant in Captain Thayer's company, dated March 4, 1784.

Samuel Metcalf appears on an order dated Holliston, Feb. 27, 1784, for wages for 1777–1778 and signed by himself in the 6th Mass. regiment. This record, though showing good service done by the hero through the long weary years of the war for the independence of the Colonies, reveals the fact that the country was utterly bankrupt and that it could not, if it would, make payment to its defenders against British tyranny.

PYNCHON GENEALOGY.

The following, relating to the ancient Pynchon family is taken from the New England Hist. and Gen. Reg. vol. XXXVII., page 361 and ff. :

" Pynchon Families in Springfield. 1st Generation. The Hon. Col. William Pynchon, one of the first patentees of the colony of Massachusetts and treasurer of the same, came to New England in the year 1629 with Governor Winthrop and others. In the year 1636 he, as principal leader of the first settlers, came from Roxbury to Springfield. By the public records it appears that his children, which were with him in Springfield, were : Col. John Pynchon, his successor ; the wife of Mr. Henry Smith, Mary ; the wife of Capt. Elizur Holyoke, and Margaret, who was married Dec. 6, 1644, to Mr. William Davis. By the records of the General Court of Mass., it appears that Col. William Pynchon published something which the court considered to be heritical and which gave offense. The court proposed to write to England, signifying its disapprobation of the doctrines advanced by Col. Pynchon, and they also appointed Mr. Norton of Ipswich to confute the arguments advanced by Col. Pynchon. The court also suspended him from his office at Springfield, appointing Mr. Henry Smith to succeed him. These transactions of the General Court, and some difficulties with people of Connecticut River, are supposed to have been the cause of Col. William Pynchon's leaving Springfield and Mass., as it is said he did, September, 1652, with his son-in-law, Mr. Henry Smith, and returned to England. He died in a place called Wraisbury, Oct., 1662, aged 72. The following is a reproduction of the signature of this remarkable man :

" Second Generation.—Colonel John Pynchon, of Springfield, son of Col. William Pynchon, was married Oct. 30, 1644, to Anne Willis. Their children were : Joseph, born July 26, 1646; John, born Oct. 15, 1647, died April 25, 1721 ; Mary, born Oct. 28, 1650 ; William, born Oct. 11, 1653, died June 15, 1654; Mehetabel, born Nov. 22, 1661, died July 24, 1663. Joseph, educated at Harvard College, was graduated A. D., 1664, was in England, 1675, at the time Springfield was burnt by the Indians. He settled in Boston and died unmarried. The family of John follows this. Mary was married Oct. 5, 1669, to Joseph Whitney. Mrs. Anne Pynchon the mother died Jan. 9, 1699. Col. John Pynchon the father died Jan. 17, 1703.

" Third Generation.—Col. John Pynchon, of Springfield, son of Col. John and Amy Pynchon above, was married to Margaret Hubbard, daughter of the Rev. William Hubbard, of Ipswich. His wife remained during the Indian war at Ipswich, where his children were born, and after the war they settled at Springfield. Their children were: John, born ——, died July 12, 1742 ; Margaret, born ——; William, born ——, died Jan. 1, 1741. Margaret, the daughter was married to (Captain) Nathaniel Downing, of Ipswich, and had six children, viz.: Nathaniel, John, Margaret, *Jane*, Lucy, and Anna. The families of the sons John and William, see below. Col. John Pynchon the father and his father in their day, made great improvement both in the county and town wherein they lived, as appears from records. The second Col. John Pynchon was one of the commissioners of the united colonies. He died April 25, 1721. Margaret his wife died Nov. 11, 1716."

The following relating to the Pynchon Lineage is from Dwight's Genealogy, page 628 : —

No family in the land was more conspicuous for excellence in the early days of N. E. History than the Pynchon family.

Nicholas Pynchon of Wales, Sheriff of London, in 1533, had a son, John Pynchon of Writtle, Essex, who m. Jane, heiress of Sir Richard Empson, and d. Nov. 29, 1573, leaving six children. His widow, Mrs. Jane Pynchon, m. Dr. Thomas Wilson, Secretary of State. (See Heraldic Journal, Boston, April, 1866.) Their children were :

I. William, who m. Rosa Reding of Pinner, Middlesex, England.

II. John Pynchon, who settled in Springfield, Essex, England, and was the progenitor of the American Pynchons.

III. Sir Edward Pynchon.

IV. Agnes Pynchon, who m. Thomas Chicele of Hingham, furrier.

V. Elizabeth Pynchon, who m. Geoffrey Gates of St. Edmunds Bury.

VI. Jane Pynchon, who m. Andrew Paschal, of Springfield, England.

John Pynchon of Springfield, Essex, England, had a son William Pynchon, the settler in Mass. He was one of the patentees of the colony charter of Massachusetts Bay, and was appointed magistrate and assistant in 1629, in England. He came hither in 1630, with Gov. Winthrop, and began the settlement of Roxbury, Mass., being its principal founder, and the prime mover in founding the Congregational Church established there, thus laying the foundation himself of two important American towns. In 1650, he was censured for having published a work entitled, "The Meritorious Price of Man's Redemption," and cited to appear before the court, and laid under heavy bonds. It is a dialogue in form, and is described as having been a book full of errors and weakness, and some heresy, which the General Court of Massachusetts condemned to be burned. The grand error of the book consisted, it was said, "in regarding the sufferings of Christ as merely trials of his obedience." The next year he retracted his statements, and the censure was suspended; but he was so much dissatisfied that he went back to England, and never returned to this country again. He was a man of high mark for both intellect and excellence. It was in 1652 that he left the new world, after twenty-two years' residence here, for his old home. His wife, whose name is unknown to the author, died in 1630, shortly after his arrival here; and he m. a second wife, widow, Frances Sanford, a "grave matron of the church of Dorchester," Mass. She died in England, Oct. 10, 1657; he in Wyrardisbury, England, October of 1661, aged seventy-two. His children by the first marriage were Ann, Mary, Major John, and Margaret; they all remained in this country.

Major John Pynchon (son of William Pynchon, the settler) b. in England in 1625, came to this country with his father when he was 5 years old. He m. Oct. 30, 1645, Amy Wyllys, b. in England in 1624 (daughter of Gov. Wyllys of Hartford, Ct. and Mary ——). He was a man of very superior talents, character, and social position. He represented the town of Springfield in the General Court in 1659, '62 and '63, and was for twenty-one years (1665-86) an "assistant" in it. He was spoken of and addressed by the title of "The Worshipful." From 1652 to 1660 (when Hampshire co. was incorporated) he, with two others, had a joint commission to hear and determine causes, and from 1692 to 1702 he was Chief Justice of the Court of Common Pleas for Hampshire co. He was a large farmer and landholder, and owned several sawmills and gristmills, and was much engaged in public business. Even as far off as New London, Ct., he bought 2400 acres of land, in company with James Rogers. In King Philip's War, in 1675, his brick house built, in 1660, was used as a fort for defense. At the beginning of the attack in June he was in Hadley. He died Jan. 17, 1702-3, aged seventy-six. His wife d. Jan. 9, 1698-9, aged seventy-four.

CHILDREN.—THIRD GENERATION.

Col. John Pynchon b. Oct., 15, 1647, m. about 1672, Margaret Hubbard (daughter of Rev. Wm. Hubbard of Ipswich, Mass., the N. E. Historian, and Margaret Rogers, daughter of Rev. Nathaniel Rogers of Ipswich and Margaret Crane.

He was lieut. colonel, and clerk of the Courts and register of Deeds. He lived in Boston, and afterwards at Ipswich and Springfield. He was made judge in 1708, and died April 25, 1721. (See Washburn's Judicial History, Mass.) She died at Springfield, Nov. 11, 1716. His children were all born at Ipswich.

CHILDREN.—FOURTH GENERATION.

I. Col. John Pynchon Jr., b. in 1674, d. July 12, 1742.

II. Margaret Pynchon, b. about 1680, m. Captain Nathaniel Downing.

The full and interesting record found in Savage's New England Gen. Dict., vol. 2, page 65-7, relating to the Downing family with which Margaret Pynchon became allied when she married Captain Nathaniel Downing, whose illustrious family in 1800, founded Downing College, Cambridge, England, is here produced. (New Eng. Gen. Dict. vol. 2, page 65.)

ARMS OF DOWNING.

The arms of Downing of the county, of Norfolk, England, are:—Barry of eight argent and vert, over all a griffon sejeant or.

DOWNING GENEALOGY.

"Downing, Benjamin, Hatfield 1679, took the o. of alleg. that yr. and m. the second yr. Sarah, d. perhaps eldest, of William Hunter; may have been, but prob. not, s. of Emanuel. Dennis, Kittery 1650, in Nov. 1652 sw. alleg. to Mass., and was k. by the Ind. 4 July, 1697, unless the sufferer were s. of the first. Emanuel, Salem, from London, where he was a lawyer of the Inner Temple, inhab. of the parish of St. Michael, Cornhill Ward, came in 1638 with his wife Lucy, d. of Adam Winthrop, Esqr. of Groton, in co. Suff. where she was baptized 27 Jan. 1601, sis. of our first Gov. of Mass., m. 10 Apr. 1622. They were adm. of the ch. 4 Nov., 1638, and he was sw. a freeman Mar., 1639, rep. the same yr. 40, 1, 4 and 8 ; was propos. for an Assist. in 1641, but not chos. His ch. were George, b. prob. in 1623, or 4, and was perhaps, kept in sch. at home until his f. came ; Mary, who came May, 1633 with Gov., Coddington in the "Mary and Jane," and in Nov., of that yr. was adm. of the ch. in Boston ; James, wh. was brot. by his uncle, the Gov. in the Arbella 1630 ; Susan, wh. came at the same time with Mary ; Ann ; Lucy; and these foll. b. on our side of the ocean, John, bap. 1 Mar., 1640 ; and Dorcas, 7 Feb., 1641. He went home early in 1642, back next yr. and went again in 1644, on business, but came back next yr. The date of his d. is not found, nor that of his w. tho. we see proof of his req. to the Gen. Ct. Sept., 1653 for his 600 acres to be laid out, and of her liv. 4 Aug., 1656, when she gave to Capt. Joseph Gardner dowry on his m. with her d. and the same shows that her h. Emanuel was d. The s. James, I think, liv. at Ipswich ; Mary m. Anthony Stoddard of Boston ; Ann was w. of the intrepid Capt. Gardner, k. at the gr. Narraganset swamp fight in Philip's war, and after m. Gov. Bradstreet. There was a John D. wh. d. at Boston, 29 April, 1694, but he was a merch. from Nevis, where was his fam. and est. George, Salem, s. of the preced. b. in London, was partly prepar. for coll. by Rev. John Fiske, and gr. in the first class, H. C. 1642, went to Eng. by way of New-foundland, St. Kitts, Barbadoes, and Nevis, and in each isl. was desir. to preach, but perhaps saw prospect of greater usefulness in his native land, where he bec. as his uncle Winth. tells, 1645, a chaplain in the regim. of Okey, wh. after was made one of the judges to sign the warrant for execut. of Charles I. He got forward fast (possib. faster, as Okey sunk), in favor with Cromwell, wh. made him his resident at the Hague; and in 1654 unit. with "the blood of all the How-ards" by m. with Frances, descend. thro. the sec. s. from that fourth Duke of Norfolk wh. was by Queen Eliz. behead. for ten-derness to Mary, Queen of Scots. The Hon. Charles Howard, br. of Frances, was the first, of only three, by Oliver creat. peers of Eng. under title of Viscount Morpeth. The infirmity of this honor was, soon after the restor. strengthen. by his creat. 20 Apr. 1661, as first Earl of Carlisle, wh. title is now enjoy. by his lineal heirs. Previous to this dignity conferr. on the Howard stock, and even bef. his restor. the king had made D. a knight for his good conduct in Holland; and, 1 July, 1663, he was made baronet, by the style of Sir George D. of Gamlingay, in co. Cambridge, where his est. was call. the largest in that country. His w. d. 10 July, 1683, and he d. 1684. His s. Charles was one of the tellers in the Exch. by indent. at London, 13 Sept., 1700, sold the est. at Salem, that was his gr. f'.s and to him from Emanuel had come thro. George, as in our Register of Essex co. vol. XVII. appears. His eldest s. Sir George m. Catherine, eldest d. of James, Earl of Salisbury, of the illustr. house of Cecil, and their s. Sir George after sit. in two parliaments of Queen Anne, and the first of George II. d. without issue, and left the splendid resid. devise. to the Union of Cambr. wh. laid the founda. of Downing Coll. In possess. of Dawson Turner, Esqr. F. A. S. at Great Yarmouth, is a collect. of Downing papers, in wh. some curious matter may prob. exist. I had slight inspect. of them in 1842, but look. only at the earliest, when the N. E. youth was scout-master-gen. in Scotland. A dispatch from Downing, of 3 Sept., 1651, that day of Worcester route, wh. Cromwell with proper forecast, call. his *crowning* mercy, may be read in Cary's Memorials of the civ. war, vol. II. It is far more perspicuous and soldier-like than that of the Command.-in-Chief. But the skill or valor of such a field was no longer in request, and it was to his fidel. probity, and diligence in other affairs that Oliver direct. John Milton to certify. Winth. II. 241. Hutch. I. III. John, Charlestown to his w. Joanna wh. bore him Mary, 6 Aug., 1659, d. 13 Nov. foll., was giv. admin. his est. 2 Apr., 1663. John, Wells, perhaps s. of Dennis, or br. had John, b. a 1660. John, Ipswich, m. 2 Nov. 1669, Mehetabel, d. of Richard Brabrook, had John, b. 31 Oct. 1675; Margaret, 7 Feb. 1679; and Richard, wh. d. 3 Nov. 1702. John, Braintree, 1673, was a soldier in Philip's war with Capt. Turner, in Apr., 1676, on Conn. riv. sett. at Hatfield, m. soon after, Mary, wid. of Thomas Meakins, jr. (wh. had been k. by the Ind. the yr. bef.), had Jonathan, b. 1677; and John, 1678; perhaps rem. from H. Joshua, Kittery, perhaps s. of Dennis of the same, by w. Rebecca had Eliz., b. late in the 17th centu. and perhaps others, Malcolm, Lynn, a Scotchman, m. June, 1653, Margaret Sullivan. had Mary, b. Feb., 1655; Hannah, 3 Apr., 1657; Sarah, 1 Mar., 1659: Margaret, 15 Jan., 1661; Priscilla, 15 Mar., 1662; Catharine, 15 Aug., 1665; John, 20 Nov., 1667; and Joanna, 26 Feb., 1671. Richard of Ipswich, d. 3 Nov, 1702, but I kn. nothing more of him, exc. that in 1664 (three yrs. bef. he was m.), he was 27 yrs. old, yet from seeing him among proprs. of Salem or Marblehead, 1674, hav. w. Mary, I venture to guess that he was a gr.-s. of Emanuel. Theophilus, Salem, 1642, had gr. of ld. 29 Nov. of that yr., and s. Theophilus, bapt. 13 Mar., 1642; Ann, or Hannah, 8 Sept., 1644; and Benjamin, 17 Jan., 1647; in the first two instances the ch. are noted as of our sis. D. and in the last as of Ellen D. He is call. the fisherman, and nothing more is ascert. He was of Marblehead part of the town, perhaps br. of Richard or of Malcolm, and may have had other ch. His w. may have come from some other town. William, Boston, freem. 1690.

From the New Eng. Hist. and Gen. Register, vol. 38, p. 193 is the following: —

Nathaniel Downeinge of London, gentleman, 7 May, 1616, will proved 14 May, 1616, by his wife Margaret Downeinge. To be buried in the parish church of St. Dionis Backchurch, London, or elsewhere it shall please my executrix. To the poor of St. Dionis and St. Gabriel Fanchurch, London. To my brother Joseph Downeinge, now dwelling in Ipswich, in the County of Suffolk, twenty pounds.

William H. [Richardson, Esq., F. S. A., who has annotated " The Annals of Ipswiche, by N. Bacon," says that George Downing, who was undoubtedly the father of Emanuel and Nathaniel Downing, was master of the Grammar School, Ipswich, about the years 1607 to 1610. His son Emanuel baptized in the parish church of St. Lawrence, Ipswich, 12 August, 1585, married at Groton, Suffolk, 10 April, 1622 (Lucy baptized 27 January, 1601), daughter of Adam Winthrop, Esq., and sister of Governor John Winthrop. Mr. Emanuel Downing was a lawyer of the Inner Temple, London, Attorney in the Court of Wards, and seems to have lived in the parishes of St. Bridget and of St. Michael, Cornhill. He came over to New England in 1638, took up his abode in Salem, was admitted into the church 4 November of the same year, and frequently represented the town in the General Court of the colony. The date of his death is not known, nor has any record yet been found of any will made by him. We have seen what became of his farm in Salem. His town residence was conveyed, 8 August, 1656, by Lucie Downing of Salem, with consent of Emanuel Downing, her husband (as is cited in the deed) to their son Lieut. Joseph Gardner, as the dower of their daughter Ann on her marriage with Lieut. Gardner.

Nathaniel Downing, brother of Emanuel and uncle of Sir George, was baptized in the church of St. Mary at the Tower, Ipswich, 8 October, 1587. He married 6 May, 1613, Margaret, daughter of Doctor Daniel Selyne (or Selin), a French physician, who died 19 March, 1614-15, and in his will (Rudd., 28) mentions his son-in-law, Nathaniel Downing. Mr. Downing seems to have had one son, Daniel, baptized at St. Dionis Backchurch, 5 April, 1614, and buried five days afterwards.

The following is taken from vol. 96, page 26 and ff. ——

The town of Groton is indebted for its name to Deane Winthrop, a son of Governor John Winthrop and one of the petitioners for its incorporation. He was born at Groton, Suffolk, in Old England; and the love of his native place prompted him to perpetuate its name in New England. He stands at the head of the first list of selectmen appointed by the General Court, and for a short time was probably a resident of the town.

A few years before this time, Emanuel Downing, of Salem, who married Lucy, a sister of Governor John Winthrop, had a very large farm which he called Groton. It was situated in what was afterwards South Danvers, but now Peabody, on the old road leading from Lynn to Ipswich, and thus named — says Upham in his "History of Witchcraft" — "in dear remembrance of his wife's ancestral home in the old country" (1.43). Downing subsequently sold it to his nephews John Winthrop, Jr., and Adam Winthrop, on July 23, 1644, when he speaks of it as "his farme of Groton." The sale is duly recorded in the Suffolk Registry of Deeds (1.57). Groton in England is an ancient place; it is the same as the Grotena of Domesday Book, in which there is a record of the population and wealth of the town, in some detail, at the time of William the Conqueror, and also before him, under the Anglo-Saxon King, Edward the Confessor. A nearly literal translation of this census return of the year 1086 is as follows : —

"In the time of King Edward [the Abbot of] St. Edmund held Groton for a manor, there being one carucate and a half of land. Always [there have been] eight villeins and five bordarii [a rather higher sort of serfs; cotters]. Always [there have been] one plough in demesne. Always two ploughs belonging to homagers [tenants], and one acre of meadow. Woodland for ten hogs. A mill serviceable in winter. Always one work-house, six cattle, and sixteen hogs, and thirty sheep. Two free men of half a carucate of land, and they could give away and sell their land. Six bordarii. Always one plough, and one acre of meadow [belonging to these bordarii]. It was then [i. e., under King Edward] worth thirty shillings, and now valued at forty. It is seven furlongs in length and four in breadth. In the same, twelve free men, and they could have one carucate ; it is worth twenty shillings. These men could give away and sell their land in the reign of King Edward. [The Abbot of] Saint Edmund has the soc. protection and servitude. Its gelt is seven pence, but others hold there."

"The pedigree of the Downings is full of interest. We know that Emanuel Downing m. April 10, 1622, Lucy, sister of Gov. John Winthrop. They had a dau. Ann, who m. 1st. (the intrepid) Captain Joseph Gardner, and 2d, Gov. Simon Bradstreet, and also a daughter Lucy. Mr. Thornton, before he knew that Emanuel Downing had a daughter Lucy, conjectured, from the above will of Mrs. Anne Bradstreet, that Lucy, the wife of William Norton, was Mrs. B.'s sister; and his subsequent investigations have strengthened this opinion. It is a curious fact that though we know that the noted Sir George Downing was the son of Emanuel, [honest Antony A.] Wood ['Athenae Oxoniensis'] a contemporary, said he was the son of Calibut Downing. Again, a Baronetage, published in 1727, in the life-time of the grand-son of Sir George, pretending to particular accuracy—as the preface states that 'application has been made to every Baronet,' &c. — states that Sir George was the son of Calybut. The descent the author thus traces. Goeffrey Downing was of Poles-Beldham, co. Essex, m. Elizabeth, dau. of Thomas Wingfield, and had issue, Arthur Downing, of Lexham, co. Norfolk, where he increased his fortune by marrying Susan, daughter and co-heir of John Calybut, of Castle-Acre in that county. Their issue was Dorothy, Anne, and John. Son or brother of this John was Calibut Downing, of Shermington, co. Gloucester, who was father of the famous Rev. Calybut. This latter, as we have said before, is called the father of Sir George. The reader will note the confusion relative to the affiliation of Calibut, Sen., to the parent stem; does not this suggest a relationship of Rev. Calybut to Sir George, though the precise degree is unknown?

I learn from Henry White, Esq., of New Haven, that there was a John Downing, a merchant of Nevis, who died at Boston [April 29,] 1694, leaving a son Nathaniel, and there is strong presumptive evidence that he was a son of Emanuel Downing [the father of Sir George]."

Vol. XVII, Page 290, N. Eng. Gen. and Antiq. Reg.
Proceedings of the Mass. Hist. Soc.
"The genealogical items in these volumes are not many, but are very interesting. In the collections we find the will of Isaac Johnson,and a note on p. 40d.,by Mr. Somerby, gives the probable record of Emanuel Downing's birth from the Register of the church of St. Lawrence in Ipswich, co. Suffolk. It is, '1585, Emanuel, the son of George Downing, Capt. ye 1 of Jan.' George, the father, describes himself in his will, proved 3d Oct., 1611, as a schoolmaster of Ipswich."

Emanuel Downing rendered valuable service to the colony through his influence in England, and was largely instrumental in saving the Charter from being withdrawn when it was attacked in 1633–4 by Laud, Archbishop of Canterbury. He went to England in 1642, and returned the following year; he went again across the ocean in 1644, and returned in 1645. He probably died in England. His wife Lucy bore him three children, one of whom was named George, who became famous, or as some say, infamous. George Downing was born in England in 1623; he came to America with his parents, was educated at Harvard College, returned to England in 1645, was a preacher for a brief time, a commissary general of the Forces of the Parliamentary Army in 1653. He married Frances, daughter of Sir William Howard and sister of the Earl of Carlisle in 1654. He was member of parliament for Edinburgh 1654–1656 and ambassador for Cromwell to the Hague 1657–1660; seceded from Charles II., and was reappointed ambassador 1660. He betrayed three of the regicides to execution, March, 1662. Pepys calls him an ungrateful villain. George was knighted by Charles II., 1660, created baronet, July, 1663. He died 1684. Downing street, in London, the official residence of the prime ministers of England, was laid out after the great fire 1660, and was named after him. His sister Lucy married the Rev. William Norton, said to have been a lineal descendant of King Alfred the Great. Mary, his sister, married Anthony Stoddard of Boston.

According to Burke's Heraldry, Sir George Downing had besides his son Charles the Teller of the Exchequer, and his son Sir

George who married Catharine, eldest daughter of James, Earl of
Salisbury, of the illustrious house of Cecil, still another son,
Henry Downing in Ireland. Burke says Henry was a younger
brother of Sir George Downing, the first baronet of East Hadley,
Cambridgeshire. This is doubtful. Henry may have been a son
of Calibut Downing before mentioned. Sir George Downing, who
married Catharine, eldest daughter of James, Earl of Salisbury,
after sitting in two parliaments of Queen Anne and the first of
George II., died 1747 without issue, and left the splendid residence devised to the University of Cambridge, and thus laid the
foundation of Downing College, which is the youngest of that seat
of the muses. The value of the bequest in 1851 was 150,000
pounds.

Nathaniel Downing, who married, Aug. 10, 1704, at Ipswich,
Mass., Margaret Pynchon, daughter of Col. John^3 Pynchon and
Margaret Hubbard, daughter of the Rev. William Hubbard of
Ipswich, was the son of John Downing, the merchant of Nevis,
who was baptised on this side of the ocean in 1640, and died in
Boston, April 29, 1694. This John Downing, the merchant, the
father of Captain Nathaniel Downing, was the son of Emanuel
Downing, who was the father of Sir George Downing, as before
mentioned. Nathaniel Downing was born about 1680, probably
in Nevis, and after the death of his father became a resident of
Ipswich, Mass. He is said to have died in Springfield, Mass.

There is a record that a John Downing* and a Hannah Ridg-
away were married in Boston, Mass., Sept. 27, 1698, by Cotton
Mather. This seems not to have been the first m. of Hannah, for
according to Lewis's History of Lynn, the Rev. Jeremiah Shepard
was the fourth son of the Rev. Thomas Shepard, minister of
Cambridge, who came from Towcester in England, 1635. The
name of Shepard's wife was Mary, and she was the daughter of
Francis Wainwright of Ipswich. She, Mary (Wainwright) Shepard, died March 28, 1710, aged 53 years. He had 9 children: 1st,
Hannah, b. 1676, m. John Downing of Boston, 1698.

---

*John Downing was the son of John Downing the merchant of Nevis, and brother
of Captain Nathaniel Downing and also grandson of Emanuel Downing, whose
genealogy has been traced.

From the Register of Tonnage kept by the chief magistrate according to an Act of Parliament, for vessels owned in Ipswich, it appears that Nathaniel Downing was master of the sloop, "Seahorse," of thirty tons burden.

According to the register of the New England Historic Genealogical Society, the names of the early settlers of West Springfield appear transcribed from the parish records of the First Congregational Church, by Lyman H. Bagg. On page 50 is the following : —

"Jany. 16th 17$^{20}_{21}$. Att a meeting of the propriety It was voted that ——————— And Serja^t Bag Wm Scot and Cap^{tt} Downeing ware chosen to be the Comitey for the worck to divide the s^d land to them for whom we are to provide lots for." On page 55 is the following : —

"In the next place is an a Count of the divideing of that tier of lots on the west side of the high way or street And the Number begins from that end next dorbeys Brook going Northerly. 2. The second lot is to Cap^{tt} Nath^{ll} Downeing ten acres in length eighty Rods. In Bredth twenty Rods."

On page 286 of vol. 29, may be seen the following : —

"In the Next place a list was drawn of the Names of those that ware to be provided for who ware such as had Removed hither & ware Inhabitants or such of the Inhabitants as ware born hear and had attained to the Age of twenty-one years which was determined by a vote as followeth :" Date 1720. Among the names was that of Cap^{tt} Downeing.

The children of Capt. Nathaniel[4] (John[3], Emanuel[2], George[1]) Downing and Margaret[7] (Col. John[6], Col. John[5], William[4] the emigrant ancestor, John[3] of Springfield, Essex, Eng., John[2] of Writtle, Essex, Eng., Nicholas[1] of Wales, Sheriff of London in 1533) Pynchon were : —

Nathaniel, born in Ipswich, Mass., 5-7-1706, who seems to have died young.

Nathaniel, b. in Springfield, Mass., Feb. 22, 1710-11.

John, b. in Springfield, Mass., July 15, 1712.

Margrett, b. in Springfield, Mass., March 23, 1714.

Jane, b. in Springfield, Mass., July 19, 1716.

Luci, b. in Springfield, Mass., Nov. 20, 1720 or
Lucy, b. in Springfield, Mass., Nov. 19, 1720 (two records).
Ann, b. in Springfield, Mass., Nov. 11, 1723.

Also a record of the death of a daughter, Margaret Downing, July 15, 1710, and that "Capt. Nathan" Downing had a daughter, died May 10, 1718."

Jane Downing, the daughter of Capt. Nathaniel Downing above mentioned, was the mother of Mrs. Hannah Richardson, wife of Mr. Thomas Richardson of Rutland, Mass., and grandmother of Mrs. Jane Metcalf Orne, and great grandmother of Mrs. Hannah Orne Gray, and great great grandmother of Mrs. Mary Hannah Gray Clarke, and great great great grandmother of Inez Louise and Genevieve Clarke, of Cambridge, Mass.

The following is a copy of the will of John Downing, Merchant of Nevis, who died in Boston, April 29, 1694, and the inventory of his estate, found in the Suffolk Co. Probate Records at the New Court House in Boston, Mass., Vol. XIII.—pp. 461 and 533.

WILL OF JOHN DOWNING.

In the name of God Amen the seventh day of February Anno Dom¹. one thousand six hundred and ninety-91 Annoque R. R⁵. et Reginæ Guilielmi et Mariæ nunc Angliæ &cᵃ Secundo. I John Downing of the Island of Nevis in the West Indies, at present sojourning at Boston in New England being in good bodily health and of sound mind and memory, praised be Almighty God for the same,

Knowing the uncertainty of this present life and being desirous to settle that outward Estate the Lord hath lent me, Do therefore make and ordaine this my last Will and Testament in manner following. That is to say. First and principally I commend my Soul into yᵉ hands of God my Creator hopeing to receive full pardon and remiffion of all my sins, and salvation through the alone merits of Jesus Christ my Redeemer, and my body to the Earth to be buried in decent mannʳ according to the discretion of my Executors or one of them herein named. And touching such wordly Estate the Lord hath lent me. My will and meaning is, the same shall be imployed and bestowed as hereafter in and by this my Will is exprest.

Imprimis I hereby revoke, renounce and make void all Wills and Testaments by me heretofore made, and declare and appoint this to be my last Will and Testament, Item I Will, that all the Debts that I justly owe to any manner of person or persons whatsoever, shall be well and truely paid, or ordained to be paid in convenient time next after my decease, by my Executors, or one of them hereafter named. Item after my Debts and Funeral Expences are paid and satisfied. I do hereby give, devise, and bequeath all that my Meffuage or Tenement, with all the Land thereunto belonging, scituate in Nevis afores^d (wherein my son Charles Downing dece^d. formerly inhabited) unto my Child by the said Charles in his lifetime by him begotten, on the body of Susanna his late wife, and borne to be born of her, and to the heirs and affignes forever of s^d. Child, if it live to attaine the age of Twenty-one yeares. Item I do hereby give, devise and bequeath my other houseing, Meffuage or Tenement with all the Lands, yards, Garden, profits, priviledges and appurtenances thereto belonging scituate, lying and being in Nevis afores^d. now or late in my own improvement, Together with all Household Goods, moveables, Debts and other Estate whatsoever either real or personal unto my two sons vizt. John Downing of Nevis————— and Nathaniel Downing residing now in Boston aboves^d. and to their heires, and affignes for ever in equal halves. Item My Will is that my Son Nathaniel shall have the Charges of his Education in bringing him up to be a Scholar, discharged out of my Estate, before Division thereof be made, and until division thereof be made its my Will that my Son John do live thereupon, and husband the same to as little wast as may be. Item It is my Will that when my Son Nathaniel attaines the age of Twenty-one yeares — or be married, which of them first happens an equal Division of my s^d. Estate shall be made between my Son John & Nathaniel. Item if it should so happen that all my Children dye without issue, leaving all or any part of my afores^d. Estate undisposed of by them, Then in such Case I do hereby give. devise and bequeath the same as followeth Viz^t. One Third part thereof & y^e.

Children of the Reverend M^r. Samuel Willard Teacher of a Congregation appertaining or belonging to the third (or South) Meeting house (so called) in Boston aboves^d. one third part more thereof to the Children of my Kinsman Elizur Holyoke of Boston -afores^d. Merch^t. and to ye heires and affignes for ever of the aforementioned Children, and the remaining third part thereof, to the poor of the aforesaid South Church. Item I do hereby constitute and appoint my Sons the s^d. John and Nathaniel to be the Executors of this my last Will and Testament, and do desire and entreat my good Friends Deacon Jacob Eliott and the s^d Elizur Holyoke of Boston afores^d. and Solomon Israel and Francis Teepe of Nevis, to be the Overseers thereof, requesting them to affist my Executors in the due performance of this my s^d. Will, unto whome I give Forty Shillings apiece, as a Token of my love. Item my Will is, That if the within mentioned Susanna be not left with Child by my dece^d. Son, Then my first mentioned Meffuage or Tenement shall be equally divided, amongst my other two sons, and their Heires according as is herein before declared. In Witness whereof I have hereunto set my hand and Seal the day and yeare first within written — John Downing and a Seal. Signed, Sealed, published and declared by the s^d. John Downing as his last Will and Testament in presence of us William Crow; W^m: Gilbert Jun^e. Edward Oakes. Eliezer Moody. Scr. Exam^d. P.^{r} Is^c. Addington Esqr.

The Inventory of the Estate of John Downing dece^d. taken this 18th day of January, 1694, and apprized by Elizur Holyoke and Samuel Wentworth Imp^s.

In money £1658,,11,,2 (£ 76,,10,,—whereof being for a Sloop sold

& her Freight home)	£1658,,11,,2
2 Seals & 3 hoop rings qt. 1 oz. 19 gr: at 5^p P.oz	5 4 —
3 Ps of Gold 3^p,,1^s ,,9. A Silver cup and bodkin 5-6d . . .	3 7 3
Apparrell woollen and linnen	16 — —
a bedtick, bolster and 3pr pillowticks	3 — —
2 pair Holland Sheets	2 — —
a callico counterpan and head cloth	1 10 —
31^r Pewter at 1-6s P^p	2 6 6
a Bellmettle mortar and pestle	18 —
28 Books great and small	4 10 —

Silver Scales and Weights	6 —
a gun, Cartuse box and a Sword	1 10 —
3 Table cloths 12⁵ 2 dozᶜⁿ Napkins 24	1 16 —
3 yards Kersey 20⁵ a coverlid 10ˢ	1 10 —
10 pillow cases and 1 Towell	12 —
3 brass candlesticks 6ˢ . 3 chests and a cedar box 30ˢ	1 16 —
1 Razour and hone	4 —
2 Houses at Nevis	1705 — 11

ELIZUR HOLYOKE,
SAMˡˡ· WENTWORTH.

The above is a full and true Inventory of all the Estate of my
late Father John Downing deceased, so far as hath come to my
knowledge

Presented by me

John Downing Executor.

Examᵈ P.—   Isᵃ Addington Esqʳ

Robert Gray, discoverer, mentioned on pages 87, 88 and 89, was born at Tiverton, R. I., May 10, 1755. He participated in the naval service of the War of the Revolution. In 1787 he commanded the sloop Washington, which, in company with the ship Columbia, was fitted out by merchants of Boston for the purpose of trading with the natives of the Pacific coast. The vessel set sail 30th September, but soon after doubling Cape Horn became separated from the Columbia, by the fierce storms that were then raging ; Gray's ship reached the American coast in the 46° north, August, 1788, and entered Nootka Sound, Vancouver's Island, in the month following. At this place the Columbia arrived soon after. From 1788 to 1799 Gray made further explorations, including Queen Charlotte Islands, discovered the Straits of Fuca and the mouth of the river. He returned in the ship Columbia to Boston, sailing by the way of Canton, China, in 1790, and, as before stated, was the first man to circumnavigate the world under the flag of the United States. In 1791 Gray revisited the north-west coast, where he further explored the Columbia river, giving it the name of his vessel, and returning to Boston by his former route. He was married on Feb. 4, 1794, and died, while in command of a coasting vessel, at Charleston, S. C. In 1846 the Congress of the United States granted Martha Gray, his widow, a pension for his service as soldier and discoverer. He died 1806.

(See the National Cyclopædia of Am. Biog. vol. 5, p. 121, 1896.)

Robert Gray was the son of William Gray and Elizabeth his wife, of Tiverton, R. I., whose children were : —

Phebe, b. June 29, 1741.

John, b. Feb. 13, 1743.

Lydia, b. Sept. 27, 1744.

William, b. May 1, 1747.

Mary, b. July 14, 1750.

Isaac, b. June 10, 1752.

Robert, b. May 10, 1755.

Hannah, b. July 7, 1757.

William Gray, the father of Robert, was the son of *Edward Gray and Mary* Manchester, his second wife, of Tiverton, R. I., whose children are mentioned on pp. 75, 76, 79, and 80. Edward Gray of Tiverton, it will be remembered, was the son of Edward of Plymouth, the emigrant ancestor (Robert[1], William[2], Edward[3], Edward[1]).

INDEX.

A.

B.

C.

H.

M.

174 INDEX.

Allen, Christian, of Swansey, Mass., wife of Lieutenant and Deacon Nathaniel[2] Peck, married March 8, 1695-6; died Nov. 10, 1743. He was son of Nathaniel[2] Peck and was born July 26, 1690; died August 5, 1751.

Deliverance, wife of Nathaniel[2] Peck, was buried May 1, 1675. Nathaniel[2] Peck was son of Joseph[1] Peck, emigrant ancestor, and was born at Hingham, Mass., and baptized there, Oct. 31, 1641; he was buried Aug. 12, 1676.

Fish, Lucy, wife of Joel[5] Peck, was the daughter of Daniel Fish of Seekonk, Mass. She died March 26, 1864, in her 90th year. Joel[5] Peck was son of David[4] Peck and was born August 28, 1759; he died Nov. 11, 1833. Joel[5] Peck settled upon the homestead of his fathers in Barrington, R. I.

Humphrey, Sarah, wife of David[4] Peck, m. Sept. 20, 1744. David[4] Peck, son of Nathaniel[3] Peck, was born Nov., 1707, and was baptized April 17, 1709; he died March 4, 1771.

Joel[5] Peck, of Barrington, R. I., had six children :—

Horatio, b. Dec. 3, 1793.

Elnathan, b. Jan. 27, 1796.

Bela, b. Jan. 29, 1798.

Wealthy, b, Sept. 22, 1800.

Sebea, b. Jan. 25, 1803.

Fanny, b. Sept. 6, 1805.

Bethia, b. Aug. 4, 1808.

Clarissa, b. Dec. 13, 1812.

Horatio[6] Peck m. (1st) Nancy Mathewson, da. of Daniel Mathewson, of Barrington, R. I., (2nd) Martha Chace, da. of Wanton Chace, of Pawtucket, R. I., and (3rd) Martha Martin, da. of James Martin, formerly of Newport, R. I. His children were: James B., Henry C., Martha Jane, George E., Nancy Jane, Hiram F., John M., Albert S., and Horatio W.

Elnathan[6] Peck m. Mercy Martin. His child was Sarah A., b. Oct. 8, 1829, m. Benjamin Walker, of Seekonk, June 8, 1855.

Bela[6] Peck, s. of Joel[5], m. Lemyra A. Peck, da. of Ambrose Peck, of Seekonk, Mar. 18, 1821. His children were: Alpheus M., Edwin F., Albert H., Susan A., Albert H., Horace M., Horace T., and Annie A. M.

Sebea[6] Peck, son of Joel[5], m. Rebecca Cooper, of Boston. His children were: Ann Eliza, Emily F., Seraphina M., Horatio N., and Laura Elizabeth.

Wealthy[6] Peck m. Nathaniel Medbery, of Barrington. Her children were: Matthew, Lucy, Andrew, Theophilus, Angeline, and James.

Fanny[6] Peck m. Seth Darling Clarke (see pages 24, 31-40).

Bethia[6] Peck m. Benjamin B. Medbery. Her children were: Benjamin T., Mary, Horace, and Charles.

Clarissa[6] Peck m. Robert T. Smith; no children.

Thomas Ellis was a brother of John, and came from Dedham to Medfield in the end of 1651, or the beginning of 1652. His grant for a house-lot was on North Street, the spot now occupied by his lineal descendants. The estate has never been out of the possession of the family. His house was evidently built as early as 1653, and he married in 1657 Mary Wight. He died in 1690, and his wife in 1693. Children:—

Judith, 1658; m. in 1678 Benjamin Rockwood.

Mary, 1660–1717; m. in 1678 Jonathan Adams.

Abiel, 1662–1716; m. in 1683 Zachary Barber.

Samuel, 1664.

Thomas, 1666–1670.

Patience, 1668–1695; m. in 1691 Henry Adams.

Ruth, 1670; was living unmarried in 1697.

Joanna, 1677; m. in 1698 Nathaniel Rockwood.

(See Tilden's Hist. Med.)

Joshua Darling, son of Samuel[3] (John[2], Denice[1]) and Mary Thompson his wife, m. Martha Wilson. Their children b. in Bellingham were: —

Philla, b. March 27, 1763.

Ahimas, b. March 19, 1765.

Abijah, b. April 2, 177.

Amasa, b. April 30, 1769.

Paty, b. Nov. 29, 1770.

Michael, b. Feb. 20, 1773.

William, b. Sept. 30, 1780.